JAMES MONROE
1758-1831

Chronology-Documents-Bibliographical Aids

Edited by
IAN ELLIOT

Series Editor
HOWARD F. BREMER

Oceana Publications, Inc.
Dobbs Ferry, New York 10522
1969

Library of Congress Catalog Card Number 69-15393
Oceana Book No. 303-10

Printed in the United States of America

CONTENTS

90968

Editor's Foreword

CHRONOLOGY

DOCUMENTS

BIBLIOGRAPHICAL AIDS

NAME INDEX

EDITOR'S FOREWORD

Every attempt has been made to cite the most accurate dates in this Chronology. Diaries, documents, and similar evidence have been used to determine the exact date. If, however, later scholarship has found such dates to be obviously erroneous, the more plausible date has been used. Should this Chronology be in conflict with other authorities, the student is urged to go back to original sources, as well as to such competent scholars as Stuart Gerry Brown and George Dangerfield.

This is a research tool compiled primarily for the student. While it does make some judgments on the significance of the events, it is hoped that they are reasoned judgments based on a long acquaintance with American History.

Obviously, the very selection of events by any writer is in itself a judgment.

The essence of this series of books is that many pertinent facts and key documents are made available to the student, as well as a critical bibliography which should direct him to investigate additional and/or contradictory material. The works cited may not always be available in small libraries; however, a surprisingly large percentage will be. Documents in this volume are taken from: James D. Richardson, ed., **Messages and Papers of the Presidents,** Vol. II, **Washington, 1897;** and Stanislaus Murray Hamilton, ed., **The Writings of James Monroe,** Vol. I-VII, **New York,** 1891.

CHRONOLOGY

1758

April 28

Born, Westmoreland County, Virginia. Father; Spence Monroe. Mother: Elizabeth Jones Monroe.

1769

During this year, and for approximately three subsequent years, attended school in Westmoreland County kept by Parson Archibald Campbell. During at least one of these years, his classmate in Parson Campbell's school was John Marshall, who was to serve as Chief Justice of the U.S. Supreme Court from 1801 to 1835.

1774

September

Entered William and Mary College in Williamsburg, Virginia. Father died late in year and his uncle, Judge Joseph Jones, paid his expenses. The town of Williamsburg was colonial capital of Virginia and was one of the centers of Revolutionary thought and action in the colonies.

1775

April 20

One night following the Battle of Lexington, Lord Dunmore, the Governor of Virginia, seized all of Williamsburg's gunpowder to forestall a local uprising. Williamsburg citizens and students of William and Mary College— Monroe almost certainly among them—protested en masse.

June 24

Was one of 24 men who entered the Governor's Palace— Lord Dunmore having fled to a nearly British ship—and removed all of the arms stored there.

September 28

Commissioned a second lieutenant in the Third Virginia Regiment, stationed in Williamsburg.

1776

June 24

Appointed first lieutenant in the Third Virginia Regiment. Although still in Williamsburg, he had dropped out of William and Mary College several months earlier to devote his full energies to the cause of the Revolution.

August

Left Williamsburg with his regiment to join General George Washington in New York.

1

September 16 Fought in Battle of Harlem Heights, one day after finally joining Washington's forces in New York. British attack repulsed.

October 28 Fought in Battle of White Plains. Washington withdrew to north and then across Hudson River to New Jersey.

December 25 Was among the first of Washington's troops to cross the ice-choked Delaware River at Trenton, New Jersey, to surprise the British Hessians.

December 26 Fought in the Battle of Trenton, in which 1,000 British prisoners were taken. He was severely wounded by enemy gunfire, which severed an artery in his shoulder. For "bravery under fire" during this battle, he was promoted to captain by Washington.

1777

September 11 Fought at Brandywine Creek, outside Philadelphia. During this battle—which is generally regarded as a minor defeat for Washington's forces—the Marquis de Lafayette was wounded. Monroe ministered to him, thus beginning a lifelong friendship between the two men.

October 4 Fought at Germantown, Pennsylvania.

November 20 Promoted by Washington to position of official aide-de-camp to Major General Lord Stirling, with rank of major. Stirling, who was the American William Alexander, had assumed the title of Lord.

1778

June 28 Acted as scout for Washington in Battle of Monmouth, New Jersey. When one of General Stirling's aides was badly wounded, Monroe took over and acted as Stirling's adjutant general during the rest of the engagement.

1779

May 30 Recommended by Washington for a military command to be raised by the State of Virginia. Although Monroe was appointed a lieutenant colonel of a Virginia regiment of militia, the state's exhausted finances prevented the actual raising of such a group. Monroe decided to remain in Williamsburg and study law with Thomas Jefferson.

1780

June 16   Appointed military commissioner from Virginia to the Southern Army. His duties consisted of establishing communications between Governor's Council and Southern troops.

December 20   Resigned as military commissioner.

1782

October 21   Elected member of Virginia House of Delegates.

1783

June 6   Elected a delegate from Virginia to the Fourth Congress of the Confederation, his term to begin November 3, 1783.

December 13   Took seat in Congress at Annapolis.

1784

March 22   Signed—along with Jefferson and other Virginians—a public document on the distribution of public lands, which was delivered to the Virginia Assembly. Among the more important provisions of the document: a division of territory into distinct states; states to have a republican form of government; no citizenship for persons holding "any hereditary title"; neither slavery nor involuntary servitude after 1800, except as punishment.

July 22   Set out on tour of northwest frontier to determine what type of government Congress should establish for frontier lands.

October 30   Arrived in Trenton, New Jersey, after inspection tour, in time for the opening of Congress.

1785

March 28   Recommended an amendment to Congress which would permit Congress to regulate commerce, but would leave the imposts to be collected under the authority of the state. He did not press this strongly, however.

July 20   Agreed, as member of Congressional committee, to confer upon John Jay, the secretary for foreign affairs, "the power to negotiate treaty with Don Diego de Gardoqui," the Spanish envoy. Jay was instructed to negotiate a boundary with Spain and, particularly to insist on free navigation to the north on the Mississippi.

August 25	Elected chairman of a committee dealing with negotiations for the free navigation of the Mississippi.

1786

February 16	Married in New York, N.Y., to Elizabeth Kortright, daughter of Captain Lawrence Kortright and Hannah Aspinwall Kortright of New York, N.Y.
May 10	Elected chairman of a Congressional committee to form a temporary government for the western lands.
May 15	Presented letter of resignation to Congress.
October	Admitted to the Bar of the Courts of Appeal and Chancery in Virginia; practiced law at Fredericksburg, Virginia.
December	Daughter, Eliza Kortright Monroe, born.

1787

April	Admitted to the Bar of the General Court in Virginia.

1788

June 2	Elected delegate to Virginia state convention to ratify the Federal Constitution. Opposed the Constitution originally because it gave too much power to the central government.

1789

April 30	George Washington inaugurated as the first President of the United States; John Adams, Vice-President.

1790

December 6	Took seat in the First Congress as United States Senator from Virginia. He had been elected to the office by the Virginia legislature despite the opposition of the Federalists, including his boyhood friend, John Marshall.

1791

February 21	Proposed, as Senator, that the doors of the Senate be open to the public, except on such days when secrecy is required; also proposed that a gallery be erected for the public. Monroe's proposal was adopted by the Senate almost exactly three years later. On February 20, 1794, Senate sessions became open to the public.

1792

December 5	Washington unanimously elected President for a second term.

December 15	Alexander Hamilton, then Secretary of the Treasury, informed Monroe, and two other members of Congress, of his version of the "Reynolds affair." Briefly, the situation was this: James Reynolds and Jacob Clingman were being prosecuted for criminal speculations in government funds. The two men hinted broadly that Reynolds had highly damaging information about Hamilton. Forced to defend himself against the rumors, Hamilton told Monroe what this "damaging information" was. It was simply that Hamilton had been carrying on a love affair with Reynolds' wife. (This was the beginning of a lengthy and bitter feud between Hamilton and Monroe; at one point, the two men were on the verge of dueling—see July 11, 1797.)

1793

January 2	Wrote document about Reynolds affair, in which Clingman is quoted to the effect that Mrs. Reynolds had denied all complicity. According to Monroe, this document was left "sealed with his friend in Virginia"—never identified but almost certainly Thomas Jefferson.
March 4	Washington inaugurated at Philadelphia for a second term.

1794

April 8	Wrote letter to President Washington protesting the possibility that Hamilton would be appointed envoy to Great Britain. Monroe based his opposition on the grounds that Hamilton—and Federalists generally—were too pro-British. This was the first instance of a Senator criticizing a nomination before its formal submission to the Senate.
May 27	Ended term as Senator from Virginia.
May 28	Appointed by Washington to be Minister Plenipotentiary to France. The French had demanded the recall of the Federalist, Gouveneur Morris, and Washington hoped to placate the French by appointing a Republican.
June 18	Sailed for France with his family.
August 2	Arrived in Paris at a critical point in the French Revolution. Robespierre, virtual dictator of France and the man most responsible for the Reign of Terror, fell just five days earlier.

August 13	Impatient at the seeming indifference of the French government, sent letter to the National Convention, asking to be received as the American minister.
August 15	Officially received by the National Convention. In his speech to the Convention Monroe warmly endorsed France, thus causing displeasure in England and in Federalist circles in the United States. For this speech, Monroe was sent a letter of "censure" by Secretary of State Edmund Randolph, who reminded Monroe of the United States' desire to maintain neutrality.
September 3	Requested—very mildly—that France honor two provisions of the Treaty of 1778, which prohibited the seizure (by the French) of provisions and British goods aboard American ships. Washington and Randolph were both provoked by the fact that Monroe did not demand French compliance.
November 4	Secured release of Thomas Paine, who had been imprisoned in Luxembourg Prison for more than ten months by the French revolutionists. Paine, who had taken part in the French Revolution, had been jailed for vehemently protesting the execution of the French king. After his release, he lived with Monroe and his family in Paris, for about 18 months.
November 9	Jay Treaty signed with Great Britain. Although the treaty covered many points of amity, commerce and navigation, it did not require the British to renounce right of search or imprisonment. Monroe was unsympathetic to the treaty and failed to defend it to the French.

1795

January 22	Arranged for the release of the Marquis de Lafayette's wife from La Force Prison in Paris.
April 25	New British Orders in Council authorized the seizure by British vessels of provisions on American vessels bound for French ports.
October 27	Thomas Pinckney, American envoy to Spain, negotiated the Treaty of San Lorenzo with Spain. The treaty settled the disputed boundary on the Mississippi and obtained

certain navigation rights on the Mississippi for the United States.

1796

June 13   Secretary of State Edmund Randolph wrote Monroe criticizing him for not taking all possible steps that might lead to an end to French criticisms of the Jay Treaty.

July 7   Informed by the French Minister of Foreign Affairs that France considered the United States to have abandoned neutrality with the Jay Treaty and that, therefore, the Treaty of 1778 with France was suspended.

August 22   Recalled as Minister to France for alleged failure to press American interests in France. His successsor, Charles C. Pinckney, was appointed September 9, 1796.

December 11   Received note from French Minister of Foreign Affairs in which France stated her refusal to receive Pinckney— or any other American Minister—until France received redress of her grievances.

December 30   Took formal leave of France.

1797

February 8   John Adams elected President and Thomas Jefferson Vice President.

March 4   Adams inaugurated second President of the United States.

July 11   Longstanding feud with Alexander Hamilton broke out into the open, with Hamilton blaming Monroe for the release of information about the "Reynolds affair"— particularly the document written on January 2, 1793. Monroe denied responsibility.

August 9   Received letter from Hamilton in which the latter disavowed any intention to challenge Monroe to a duel; tempers cooled on both sides.

December 2   Published a 100-page tract—known as *A View of the Conduct of the Executive* —giving his version of his recall as Minister to France and violently criticizing President Washington.

1799

May

Son born. Exact date and name unknown. A sickly child, he lived a little over two years.

December 6

Elected Governor of Virginia.

December 14

George Washington died in Mount Vernon.

1801

March 4

Thomas Jefferson inaugurated President.

September 28·

Son died.

1803

Daughter, Maria Hester, born.

January 12

Appointed by Jefferson as a minister to France to aid R.R. Livingston acquire the right of free navigation in the Mississippi River.

April 12

Arrived in Paris. Livingston had already been offered the whole province of Louisiana.

May 2

Signed, with R.R. Livingston, the Louisiana Purchase, whereby France transferred a vast area of western lands in return for 60 million francs and payment by the United States of debts incurred by France to United States citizens. The total cost to the United States was 15 million dollars.

July 12

Ended role as Minister Plenipotenitary to France, having been appointed Minister to England on April 18 to try to secure a shipping treaty.

July 18

Arrived in London.

1804

May 14

Lewis and Clark left St. Louis to conduct an overland expedition to find the headwaters of the Missouri River. They did not return until September 23, 1806.

October 4

Left London for Spain.

1805

January 2

Reached Madrid. His mission was to assist Charles Pinckney and to persuade Spain to give up, or sell, West Florida—an area not covered in the Louisiana Purchase.

January 28   With Pinckney, presented the Spanish government with a proposal by which Spain was to acknowledge the Perdido as the eastern boundary of Louisiana; Spain showed no eagerness to come to terms.

May 21   Left Spanish court for London.

July 23   Arrived in London on the day of the **Essex** decision. This case changed earlier policy about "broken voyages" and the British began to seize American ships, often outside United States harbors.

1806

May 12   Commissioned—with William Pinkney—to negotiate a treaty with England. He was instructed to secure, among other things, the end to the practice of impressment and the restoration of the principle of "broken voyages."

December 31   Concluded treaty with Britain. Although the treaty provided for certain commercial and trade concessions, it failed to come up with any arrangement on impressment, the topic uppermost in the minds of the United States statesmen. The treaty was deemed so unsatisfactory, by President Jefferson and Secretary of State Madison, that it was never submitted to the Senate.

1807

June 22   American ship of war, *Chesapeake*, fired on by British cruiser, *Leopard*, after refusing British demand to board for impressment. Three Americans were killed and 4 alleged deserters removed after boarding.

October 29   Left England for the United States.

December 13   Arrived at Norfolk, going on to Washington to report to Madison who largely ignored him.

December 22   Congress passed Jefferson's Embargo Act, which, in effect, cut off all American trade with Europe.

1808

January 21   Nominated for President by a caucus of the Virginia legislature. Monroe was supported by the "Old Republican" faction led by John Randolph of Roanoke and John Taylor of Caroline.

January 23   Congressional caucus of Democratic-Republicans nomin-
              ated James Madison for President. Monroe received only
              3 votes (as did George Clinton of New York) to 83 for
              Madison.

February 28   At a meeting with Secretary of State Madison, Monroe
              defended the rejected treaty with Britain as the best
              possible under the circumstances.

April 5   Wrote a defense of his diplomacy in England.

September   Submitted his correspondence with Randolph to President
              Jefferson to prove he was not guilty of duplicity. Monroe
              was aligning himself with the Administration in spite of
              their rejection of his diplomatic efforts.

October 17   Daughter, Eliza Kortright Monroe, married to George
              Hay.

1809

March 1   Non-intercourse Act replaced Embargo Act. It would re-
              open trade except with England and France, and with
              either or both of these if they would agree to respect
              American rights.

March 4   James Madison inaugurated as fourth President of the
              United States. Monroe, still regarded with suspicion by
              Madison and Jefferson, was omitted from the cabinet.

1810

February   Monroe, busying himself with private affairs at Albemarle,
              was visited by Thomas Jefferson and offered the governor-
              ship of Louisiana. Monroe refused, wanting an elective
              office or the post of Secretary of State.

May 1   Non-intercourse Act repealed and replaced with Macon's
              Bill No. 2. It reopened trade with England and France,
              but provided for non-intercourse against one should the
              other revoke its orders or decrees.

1811

January   Became Governor of Virginia for a second time.

March   Offered the office of Secretary of State by President Madi-
              son. Demanded a free hand in arriving at a conciliation
              with Great Britain and Madison accepted Monroe's terms.

April 2	Appointed Secretary of State by Madison to succeed Robert Smith; entered upon his duties April 6.
July 2	Appearance of new British minister, A.J. Foster, indicated little hope of Britain yielding on essential points and Monroe turned from conciliation to resistance and eventually war.
November 4	Twelfth Congress opened. British ships, at the time, were blockading the New York harbor and stopping American ships and impressing American seamen in sight of land.
November 7	General W.H. Harrison—later to become the 9th President—defeated Indian attackers under Tecumseh at Tippecanoe on the Wabash River. The event, with many American casualties, stirred up much sentiment in the West to take Canada from the British. Monroe, however, was more interested in events to the South, independence movements in Mexico for instance, and in acquiring Florida.

1812

May 14	Issued instructions—as Secretary of State—to Alexander Scott, who had recently been appointed American agent to Venezuela: "The United States are disposed to render to the Government of Venezuela, in its relations with Foreign Powers, all the good offices that they may be able. Instructions have been already given to their Ministries at Paris, St. Petersburg and London, to make known to these Courts that the United States takes an interest in the independence of the Spanish Provinces."
June 16	British Parliament suspended Orders in Council. This was, in effect, a complete capitulation to the United States; however, because of the poor communications of the time, war was nevertheless declared, by the United States, two days later.
June 18	Congress declared war against Great Britain, with much Federalist opposition.
July 26	Authorized the United States **charge d'affaires** in London to propose a suspension of hostilities if Great Britain would agree informally to suspend impressment and blockades.

August 16   General Hull surrendered Detroit to the British without firing a gun. Madison suggested that Monroe take command in the West, but finally, did not dare to put him over the West's own William Henry Harrison.

August 29   British Foreign Secretary Castlereagh rejected Monroe's armistice bid, refusing to concede the rights to impressment.

1813

January 1   Appointed Secretary of War, **ad interim;** served until February 5. Madison was replacing Secretary William Eustis with John Armstrong.

November 4   Received letter from Castlereagh offering direct peace negotiations with the United States.

1814

January 5   Wrote Castlereagh that President Madison, while preferring mediation by the Czar of Russia, would accept direct negotiations and would name commissioners to proceed to Sweden (eventually to Ghent, Belgium).

August 24   Left Washington, D.C., to join the Maryland militia at Bladensburg. The militia was forced to retreat before an overwhelming British force.

August 25   Washington, D.C. burned by the British. Monroe persuaded Madison to relieve Armstrong and give him the post of Secretary of War.

September 12-13   Francis Scott Key composed the "Star Spangled Banner" while watching an unsuccessful British attack on Fort McHenry in Baltimore.

September 27   Appointed Secretary of War on retirement of Armstrong; entered upon duties October 1, assuming the dual role of Secretary of State and of War.

December 24   Treaty of Ghent was signed by Britain and the United States, bringing to an end the War of 1812. Although the provisions of the treaty included the return of captured territory, the appointment of commissions to settle the disputed northeastern boundary, and steps toward the abolition of slave trade, there was nothing about impressment, right of search, blockade, neutral rights or indemnities, fisheries or navigation of the Mississippi.

1815

January 8   Andrew Jackson defeated the British at the Battle of New Orleans. News of the Ghent treaty did not arrive until several weeks later.

February 15   Senate unanimously ratified Treaty of Ghent.

March 14   Terminated duties as Secretary of War, having served with what is usually regarded as energy and purpose.

1816

December 4   Monroe elected fifth President. Electoral vote gave Monroe (Democratic-Republican) 183 votes, 16 States and 84.33% of the votes. His Federalist opponent, Rufus King of New York, received 34 votes, 3 States and 15.65% of the votes. Daniel D. Tompkins of New York, was elected Vice-President.

December 11   Indiana was admitted as the 19th State.

December 25   American Colonization Society formed to settle free Negroes in Africa. (See August 15, 1824.)

1817

March 3   Ended term as Secretary of State.

FIRST TERM

March 4   Inaugurated as fifth President of the United States. The oath of office was administered by his boyhood friend, John Marshall, now Chief Justice. It was the first Inauguration to be held outdoors—as a result of a controversy between the Senate and the House over the distribution of seats, the ceremonies were held on a platform erected on the east portico of the Capitol. More than 30 Inaugurations have since been held on the east portico.

March 5   Appointed John Quincy Adams of Massachusetts as Secretary of State; Adams entered upon his duties on September 22, 1817. Richard Rush of Pennsylvania, continuing as Attorney General, assumed the State office until then.

               Recommissioned William Harris Crawford of Georgia as Secretary of Treasury, the same cabinet post he had held under Madison. Also Jonathan Meigs, Jr. of Ohio as Postmaster General and Benjamin W. Crowinshield of Massachusetts as Secretary of the Navy.

April 28-29   Agreement signed by acting Secretary of State Richard Rush and British Minister Charles Bagot for disarmament on the Great Lakes.

May 31   Left for three and one-half month inspection tour of 13 states; even before announcing his Cabinet appointments, he had announced his intention of visiting all forts and posts along the seaboard. When he returned to Washington in September, he returned to a refurbished Presidential Mansion, complete with a heavy coat of white paint soon to be known as the White House.

July 4   Erie Canal construction began. Completed in October, 1825, the Canal was a New York State project, rather than federal.

July 8   Treaty signed with the Cherokee Indians. In return for a tract of land in Arkansas, the United States agreed to give reservation of 640 acres to every head of an Indian family, resident on the east side of Mississippi who might wish to become a United States Citizen.

July 12   The Boston **Columbian Centinel** noted the absence of party strife and called it an "Era of Good Feelings."

October 4   Louis Aury seized Amelia Island, declaring it part of the Republic of Mexico.

October 8   Appointed John C. Calhoun of South Carolina as Secretary of War.

November 13   Appointed William Wirt of Virginia as Attorney General.

November 20   First Seminole War began.

December 1   Opening of the first session of the Fifteenth Congress. Henry Clay of Kentucky re-elected Speaker of the House.

December 10   Mississippi admitted as the 20th State.

| December 23 | Acting upon Monroe's recommendation, Congress repealed internal taxes and made provision for winding up direct taxes. |

December 26 Secretary of War Calhoun, under authority of the President, ordered Andrew Jackson to attack the Seminole Indians.

1818

January 6 Andrew Jackson wrote confidential letter to Monroe, stating his belief that East Florida should be seized and held as indemnity for Spanish outrages on United States property. In order not to implicate the United States, Jackson suggested that Monroe give him authority by means of a letter sent to J. Rhea, a disinterested third party. The Rhea Letter, as the episode came to be known, soon became a source of great controversy and confusion. At issue was whether Monroe had given authority to Jackson and whether, indeed, he had even read Jackson's original letter.

January 13 Announced to Congress that Amelia Island had been suppressed "without the effusion of blood."

March 7 Jackson captured St. Marks, Florida, and defeated the Seminoles.

March 25 Sent message to Congress outlining state of affairs in Florida and justifying use of American troops in Spanish territory on the ground that Spain had failed to restrain Indian attacks as she was bound to do by treaty.

April 4 Flag of the United States established by Congress.

April 16 Rush-Bagot agreement (April 28-29, 1817) became treaty after Monroe had sent it to Senate and received its consent.

April 20 Tariff bill increased rates on iron products. First session of the Fifteenth Congress adjourned.

April 28 Proclaimed arrangements of April 28, 1817, between the United States and Britain, whereby each agreed to limit war vessels on Great Lakes.

April 29	Two British subjects—Alexander Arbuthnot and Robert Ambrister—executed by Jackson, after court martial found them guilty of espionage and inciting Seminoles.
May 28	Pensacola, Florida, captured by Jackson.
June 17	Spanish Minister officially protested the seizure of Spanish territory by Jackson.
July 15	Met with Cabinet to discuss dilemma the United States had been placed in by the execution of two British subjects and the capture of Spanish towns. Calhoun suggested court martial of Jackson; Adams was the general's only supporter. Three courses of action were finally decided upon: preparation of an article by Attorney General Wirt, to appear in the **National Intelligencer,** explaining to the American people what happened and offering a defense of the administration; explanation to England of why Arbuthnot and Ambrister were executed; and a reply to Spain, surrendering the captured towns and, at the same time, justifying American conduct.
October-November	The Bank of the United States (Second National Bank) being overextended in its loans began curtailing its loans and calling on its branches for specie. This caused banks to call in their own loans to farmers and speculators and to bring on a severe panic in 1819, as well as attacks on the bank, "The Monster."
October 1	Appointed Secretary of War Calhoun as ad interim Secretary of the Navy.
October 19	Treaty signed with the Chickasaw Indians, by which they ceded land between the Mississippi and the northern course of the Tennessee River.
October 20	Convention of 1818 signed at London by Richard Rush and Albert Gallatin (Minister of France). It set the 49th parallel as the boundary between the United States and British North America as far west as the Rocky Mountains.
November 9	Appointed Smith Thompson of New York as Secretary of the Navy.

November 16 Second session of the 15th Congress began.

December 3 Illinois admitted as the 21st State.

1819

February 2 John Marshall hands down decision for the Supreme Court in **Trustees of Dartmouth College v. Woodward,** with Daniel Webster having acted as attorney for the college.

February 8 Jackson vindicated by House on his Florida adventures, the opposition being led by Henry Clay. The Senate, however, condemned Jackson.

February 13 Beginning of a great controversy which culminated in the Missouri Compromise—introduction in the House of a bill permitting people of Missouri to form a state government. The bill was passed—with an anti-slavery amendment proposed by James Tallmadge of New York.

February 22 Transcontinental Treaty signed in Washington by John Quincy Adams and Don Luis de Onis, the Spanish Minister. Spain ceded East and West Florida to the United States as well as her claims to the Pacific coast north of 42°. The United States agreed to satisfy the claims of its citizens against Spain up to five million dollars.

February 25 Monroe ratified the treaty after a prompt and unaminous approval by the Senate. The King of Spain delayed ratification over a dispute about Spanish land claims, and it was not finally ratified until February 22, 1821.

February 27 Missouri bill with the Tallmadge amendment struck down by the Senate.

March 3 Authorized by Congress to restore to their own country any Africans illegally imported and seized within the United States. Also authorized to take possession of East and West Florida and establish a temporary government.

Second session of the 15th Congress adjourned.

March 6 **McCulloch v. Maryland** decision delivered by John Marshall for the Supreme Court.

March 30   Left Washington to make tour of Southern States.

May 22   "Savannah," the first American steamship to cross the Atlantic, embarked from Savannah, Georgia. The boat was toured earlier by Monroe, while on his Southern inspection trip.

December 6   First session of 16th Congress began, with Henry Clay re-elected Speaker of the House. It was the first time the two houses of Congress met in separate wings since the British burned the Capitol five years earlier.

December 14   Alabama admitted as 22nd State.

1820

March 3   Missouri Compromise passed by Congress—Maine admitted as a separate state, Missouri admitted as a slave state, and slavery prohibited in Louisiana Purchase territory, north of 36° 30'.

March 6   Signed Missouri Compromise Enabling Bill after consulting with his cabinet about its constitutionality.

March 9   Youngest daughter, Maria Hester Monroe, married Samuel Lawrence Gouveneur. This was the first wedding to take place in the White House.

March 15   Maine admitted as the 23rd State.

May 9   Delivered special message on Spanish affairs to Congress. In it, Monroe announced United States refusal to abandon the right to recognize revolutionary governments in South America.

May 15   Appointed commissioners to examine the country west of Wheeling, for the purpose of extending the Cumberland Road to the Mississippi.

First session of 16th Congress adjourned.

November 13   Second session of 16th Congress began.

December 6   Presidential election. Monroe's candidacy was unopposed.

1821

February 14 Electoral votes counted. Political differences and factions were brewing, but had not formulated. Consequently, he received all of the 232 electoral votes cast (there were 3 abstentions), with only one exception—William Plumer, Sr., of New Hampshire, one of the electors, cast his vote for John Quincy Adams. He stated that he was not opposed to Monroe, but he felt that only George Washington should have the honor of a unanimous election.

February 22 Announced acceptance by both Spain and the United States of the Florida Purchase. (See February 22, 1919.)

March 3 Second session of 16th Congress adjourned. Appointed Jackson Governor of East and West Florida.

SECOND TERM

March 5 Because March 4 fell on a Sunday, Monroe postponed the inaugural ceremonies until Monday, March 5. He took the oath of office in the Chamber of the House of Representatives because of the snow and rain. The oath was administered by Chief Justice John Marshall. This was the first postponement of an Inauguration and the first time the Marine Band played, a trend followed by all later Inaugurations.

August 10 Proclaimed the admittance of Missouri as the 24th State in the Union.

September 4 Russia issued decree, claiming the entire Pacific coast north of the 51st parallel; the decree also warned vessels of all other nations against approaching within 100 miles of the coast.

October 23 Called Cabinet meeting to discuss Jackson's dispute in Florida with Callava (former Spanish Governor) and Fromentin (American appointed judge).

December 3 Praised Jackson in annual message to Congress, but repeated confidence in Fromentin. Jackson was embittered by this.

First session of 17th Congress began.

December 31   Accepted Jackson's resignation.

1822

February 11   Russian Minister Pierre de Poletich informed Secretary of State Adams that Czar had announced Russia's claim to the Pacific Coast, from the Bering Straits to the 51st parallel north latitude. Adams replied on February 25 protesting the Russian claim.

March 8   Delivered special message to Congress, recommending the recognition of independent South American governments and asking for an appropriation for ministers to South America.

March 28   House of Representatives passed a resolution to recognize the independence of the South American republics.

May 4   Signed appropriation bill that provided $100,000 to defray the expense of "such Missions to the independent nations on the American continent" as the President might deem proper; passed with one dissenting vote.

Vetoed bill for the repair of the Cumberland Road to be paid for by tolls. His basic reason for the veto was that since violators of regulations would have to be dealt with on a Federal level, the measure would be an infringement on the police power of the states and therefore unconstitutional. On this same date, Monroe submitted a statement to Congress that called—to no avail—for an amendment that would correct this situation. Monroe basically favored internal improvements.

May 6   Authorized to appoint a Superintendent of Indian Affairs, to be resident at St. Louis.

May 8   First session of 17th Congress adjourned.

May 30   Slave insurrection in South Carolina, led by a free Negro, Denmark Vesey, subdued. 37 executed.

June 19   United States formally recognized Colombia.

December 2   Second session of 17th Congress began.

December 12   Mexico recognized by the United States.

1823

January 27	Appointed Herman Allen as first American Minister to Chile and Caesar A. Rodney as first Minister to the United Provinces of La Plata (Argentina).
January 28	Appointed James Smith Wilcocks first American Consul at Mexico City.
February 4	Authorized by Congress to tender a national ship for the voyage of Marquis de Lafayette, who was making a final visit to the United States. This offer was turned down by Lafayette.
March 3	Second session of 17th Congress adjourned.
June 26	Appointed John McLean of Ohio to be Postmaster General, to take effect on July 1.
July 17	Secretary of State Adams told Russian Minister that "We should contest the right of Russia to any territorial establishment on this continent and that we should assume distinctly the principle that the American continents are no longer subjects for any new European colonial establishments."
August 16-20	George Canning, British Foreign Secretary, proposed to Richard Rush, the United States minister in London, that a joint Anglo-American action might prevent intervention by European nations in the New World.
September 1	Appointed Secretary of the Navy Smith Thompson of New York as Associate Justice of the Supreme Court.
September 16	Appointed Lewis Southard of New Jersey as Secretary of the Navy.
October 9-12	Canning was assured by the French Minister, Prince Jules de Polignac, that France had no intention of intervening in Latin America. This is known as the Polignac Agreement. Monroe had no knowledge of it when he stated his "Doctrine" on December 2.
October 17	Monroe sent the Rush dispatches to Jefferson and Madison, asking their advice. Both favored acceptance of Canning's offer.

November 7-23   Held series of cabinet meetings on the Latin American problem. On the first day Adams argued that it would be more dignified "to avow our principles explicitly to Russia and France, than to come in as a cock-boat in the wake of the British man-of-war." Adams' advice was followed and Monroe took independent action.

November 25   Nicholas Biddle became president of the Bank of the United States.

December 2   Delivered the Monroe Doctrine in his annual message to Congress. Briefly, the Doctrine consists of two essential points: (1) "The American Continents . . . are henceforth not to be considered as subjects for future colonization by any European power"; and (2) "We should consider any attempt on their part to extend their system to any portion of this hemisphere as dangerous to our peace and safety."

1824

January 30   Advocated peace-time establishment of the Navy.

March 4   Appointed Ninian Edwards of Illinois Minister to Mexico. Edwards, a supporter of Secretary of War John C. Calhoun had written articles in 1823 attacking Secretary of the Treasury William H. Crawford. The Calhoun-Crawford feud, sparked by presidential ambitions, was symptomatic of the cabinet intrigues and the approaching end of the "Era of Good Feelings."

March 31   Henry Clay used phrase "American System" in a speech defending the protectivism in the proposed tariff.

April 17   Russia agreed, by treaty, to form no establishment on the northwest coast, south of 54° 40'. The United States agreed to make no establishment north of that line. Russia also agreed to abandon her claim of maritime jurisdiction.

April 30   Authorized by Congress, through the General Survey Bill, to use Army engineers to make the "necessary surveys, plans and estimates . . . for such a system of roads and canals as he might deem of national importance from a postal, commercial or military point of view." The bill appropriated $30,000 to permit the President to carry out this work.

August 14 Lafayette—the sole surviving general of the American Revolution—arrived in New York City, 40 years after he had taken leave of George Washington. His purpose: to make one final visit to the United States.

August 15 Upper Guinea in West Africa—which had been founded in 1817 for the purpose of colonizing free Negroes from the United States—became Liberia. The capital city was named Monrovia, in honor of President Monroe and in acknowledgement of his sympathies toward the American Colonization Society.

December 1 Presidential elections completed. The electoral votes were divided: Jackson 99, Adams 84, Crawford 41, and Clay 37. The President would be chosen from the first three by the House of Representatives.

December 10 Lafayette received in both Houses of Congress, the first man ever to have a public reception in the Senate.

1825

January 5 Presented special message to both Houses of Congress, asking for the appointment of a commission to examine his accounts and claims. Monroe had spent much of his own money during his diplomatic service in Europe. After leaving the Presidency, he was hard pressed for funds—so much so that he was forced to sell much of his property to satisfy his debts. Congress, however, was far from generous. Despite Monroe's continued claims, it was not until 1831—shortly before his death—that Congress appropriated $30,000 in partial compensation.

February 9 John Quincy Adams was elected President—over Andrew Jackson and William Harris Crawford—by vote in the House of Representatives. John C. Calhoun had been elected Vice President without difficulty.

March 3 In his final day as President, signed a bill extending the Cumberland Road from Canton to Zanesville, Ohio.

JAMES MONROE

RETIREMENT

March 23
Left Washington for his home, Oak Hill, in Loudon County, Virginia. His departure had been delayed by the illness of his wife.

July 11
Daniel D. Tompkins, Vice President under Monroe, died.

August 7
Visited at his Virginia home by Lafayette and President John Quincy Adams.

1826

July 4
Thomas Jefferson and John Adams both died.

1829

October 5
Served as chairman of the Virginia Constitutional Convention; both Madison and Marshall were members.

1830

September 23
Mrs. Monroe died at Oak Hill, Loudon County, Virginia.

November
Moved to New York City to make his home with his daughter and son-in-law, Mr. and Mrs. Gouveneur.

November 26
Presided over a meeting in Tammany Hall in New York City to celebrate the dethronement of Charles X of France. This was his last public meeting.

1831

June 19
Made deposition to the effect that he had never authorized John Rhea (see January 6, 1818) to write any letter to Andrew Jackson, authorizing him to disobey orders he had already been given in regard to Florida.

July 4
Died in New York City, five years to the day after the deaths of Jefferson and Adams. He was buried in the Gouveneur vault in New York City.

1858

July
With much ceremony on the centenary of his birth, his remains were placed on board the steamer **Jamestown** and, under the escort of the Seventh New York Regiment, were conveyed to Richmond, Virginia and re-interred in Hollywood Cemetery there.

DOCUMENTS

DEFENSE OF DIPLOMATIC MISSION
February 27, 1808

On December 31, 1806, Monroe, in his role as Minister to Great Britain, concluded a treaty with the British. Although the treaty provided for some trade and commercial concessions, it failed to deal with the topic deemed most important by American statesmen—impressment. As a result of this glaring omission, the treaty was never submitted to the Senate for approval, and Monroe, upon his return to the United States, found himself the object of much criticism. This letter to President Jefferson, written from Richmond, Va., approximately two months after his return, shows Monroe's deep bitterness at the treatment accorded him. It was a bitterness that was to rankle Monroe throughout much of his adult life.

My dear Sir,—

. . . I can assure you that no occurrences of my whole life ever gave me so much concern as some which took place during my absence abroad, proceeding from the present administration. I allude more especially to the mission of Mr. Pinkney with all the circumstances connected with that measure, and the manner in which the treaty which he and I formed, which was in fact little more than a project was received. I do not wish to dwell on those subjects. I resolved that they should not form any nature of my publick or private conduct, and I proceeded to execute my publick duty in the same manner, & to support and advance to the utmost of my power your political & personal fame, as if they had not occurred. The latter object has been felt thro' life by me scarcely as a secondary one, for from the high respect which I have entertained for your publick service, talents & virtues I have seen the natural interest, and your advancement and fame so intimately connected, as to constitute essentially the same cause. Besides I have never forgotten the proofs of kindness & friendship which I received from you in early life.

When I returned to the U States I found that heavy censure had fallen on me in the publick opinion, as I had before much reason to believe was the case, in consequence of my having signed the British treaty. And when I returned here from Washington I was assured that circumstance

with difficulties and marked by very extraordinary events the United States have flourished beyond example. Their citizens individually have been happy and the nation prosperous.

Under this Constitution our commerce has been wisely regulated with foreign nations and between the States; new States have been admitted into our Union; our territory has been enlarged by fair and honorable treaty, and with great advantage to the original States; the States, respectively protected by the National Government under a mild, parental system against foreign dangers, and enjoying within their separate spheres, by a wise partition of power, a just proportion of the sovereignty, have improved their police, extended their settlements, and attained a strength and maturity which are the best proofs of wholesome laws well administered. And if we look to the condition of individuals what a proud spectacle does it exhibit! On whom has oppression fallen in any quarter of our Union? Who has been deprived of any right of person or property? Who restrained from offering his vows in the mode which he prefers to the Divine Author of his being? It is well known that all these blessings have been enjoyed in their fullest extent; and I add with peculiar satisfaction that there has been no example of a capital punishment being inflicted on anyone for the crime of high treason.

Some who might admit the competency of our Government to these beneficent duties might doubt it in trials which put to the test its strength and efficiency as a member of the great community of nations. Here too experience has afforded us the most satisfactory proof in its favor. Just as this Constitution was put into action several of the principal States of Europe had become much agitated and some of them seriously convulsed. Destructive wars ensued, which have of late only been terminated. In the course of these conflicts the United States received great injury from several of the parties. It was their interest to stand aloof from the contest, to demand justice from the party committing the injury, and to cultivate by a fair and honorable conduct the friendship of all. War became at length inevitable, and the result has shown that our Government is equal to that, the greatest of trials, under the most unfavorable circumstances. Of the virtue of the people and of the heroic exploits of the Army, the Navy, and the militia I need not speak.

Such, then, is the happy Government under which we live—a Government adequate to every purpose for which the social compact is formed; a Government elective in all its branches, under which every citizen may by his merit obtain the highest trust recognized by the Constitution, which contains within it no cause of discord, none to put at variance one portion of the community with another; a Government which protects every citizen in the full enjoyment of his rights, and is able to protect the nation against injustice from foreign powers.

Other considerations of the highest importance admonish us to cherish our Union and to cling to the Government which supports it. Fortunate as we are in our political institutions, we have not been less so in other circumstances on which our prosperity and happiness essentially depend. Situated within the temperate zone, and extending through many degrees of latitude along the Atlantic, the United States enjoy all the varieties of climate, and every production incident to that portion of the globe. Penetrating internally to the Great Lakes and beyond the souces of the great rivers which communicate through our whole interior, no country was ever happier with respect to its domain. Blessed, too, with a fertile soil, our produce has always been very abundant, leaving, even in years the least favorable, a surplus for the wants of our fellow-men in other countries. Such is our peculiar felicity that there is not a part of our Union that is not particularly interested in preserving it. The great agricultural interest of the nation prospers under its protection. Local interests are not less fostered by it. Our fellow-citizens of the North engaged in navigation find great encouragement in being made the favored carriers of the vast productions of the other portions of the United States, while the inhabitants of these are amply recompensed, in their turn, by the nursery for seamen and naval force thus formed and reared up for the support of our common rights. Our manufactures find a generous encouragement by the policy which patronizes domestic industry, and the surplus of our produce a steady and profitable market by local wants in less-favored parts at home.

Such, then, being the highly favored condition of our country, it is the interest of every citizen to maintain it. What are the dangers which menace us? If any exist they ought to be ascertained and guarded against.

In explaining my sentiments on this subject it may be asked, What raised us to the present happy state? How did we accomplish the Revolution? How remedy the defects of the first instrument of our Union, by infusing into the National Government sufficient power for national purposes, without impairing the just rights of the States or affecting those of individuals? How sustain and pass with glory through the late war? The Government has been in the hands of the people. To the people, therefore, and to the faithful and able depositaries of their trust is the credit due. Had the people of the United States been educated in different principles, had they been less intelligent, less independent, or less virtuous, can it be believed that we should have maintained the same steady and consistent career or been blessed with the same success? While, then, the constituent body retains its present sound and healthful state everything will be safe. They will choose competent and faithful representatives for every department. It is only when the people become ignorant and corrupt, when they degenerate into a populace, that they are incapable of exercising the sovereignty. Usurpation is then an easy attainment, and an usurper soon found. The people themselves become the willing instruments of their own debasement and ruin. Let us, then, look to the great cause, and endeavor to preserve it in full force. Let us by all wise and constitutional measures promote intelligence among the people as the best means of preserving our liberties.

Dangers from abroad are not less deserving of attention. Experiencing the fortune of other nations, the United States may be again involved in war, and it may in that event be the object of the adverse party to overset our Government, to break our Union, and demolish us as a nation. Our distance from Europe and the just, moderate, and pacific policy of our Government may form some security against these dangers, but they ought to be anticipated and guarded against. Many of our citizens are engaged in commerce and navigation, and all of them are in a certain degree dependent on their prosperous state. Many are engaged in the fisheries. These interests are exposed to invasion in the wars between other powers, and we should disregard the faithful admonition of experience if we did not expect it. We must support our rights or lose our character, and with it, perhaps, our liberties. A people who fail to do it can scarcely be said to hold a place among independent nations. National honor is national property of the highest value. The sentiment in the mind of every citizen is national strength. It ought therefore to be cherished.

To secure us against these dangers our coast and inland frontiers should be fortified, our Army and Navy, regulated upon just principles as to the force of each, be kept in perfect order, and our militia be placed on the best practicable footing. To put our extensive coast in such a state of defense as to secure our cities and interior from invasion will be attended with expense, but the work when finished will be permanent, and it is fair to presume that a single campaign of invasion by a naval force superior to our own, aided by a few thousand land troops, would expose us to greater expense, without taking into the estimate the loss of property and distress of our citizens, than would be sufficient for this great work. Our land and naval forces should be moderate, but adequate to the necessary purposes—the former to garrison and preserve our fortifications and to meet the first invasions of a foreign foe, and, while constituting the elements of a greater force, to preserve the science as well as all the necessary implements of war in a state to be brought into activity in the event of war; the latter, retained within the limits proper in a state of peace, might aid in maintaining the neutrality of the United States with dignity in the wars of other powers and in saving the property of their citizens from spoliation. In time of war, with the enlargement of which the great naval resources of the country render it susceptible, and which should be duly fostered in time of peace, it would contribute essentially, both as an auxiliary of defense and as a powerful engine of annoyance, to diminish the calamities of war and to bring the war to a speedy and honorable termination.

But it ought always to be held prominently in view that the safety of these States and of everything dear to a free people must depend in an eminent degree on the militia. Invasions may be made too formidable to be resisted by any land and naval force which it would comport either with the principles of our Government or the circumstances of the United States to maintain. In such cases recourse must be had to the great body of the people, and in a manner to produce the best effect. It is of the highest importance, therefore, that they be so organized and trained as to be prepared for any emergency. The arrangement should be such as to put at the command of the Government the ardent patriotism and youthful vigor of the country. If formed on equal and just principles, it can not be oppressive. It is the crisis which makes the pressure, and not the laws which provide a remedy for it. This arrangement should be formed, too, in time of peace, to be the better prepared for war. With such an organization of such a people the United States have nothing to dread from foreign invasion. At its approach an overwhelming force of gallant men might always be put in motion.

Other interests of high importance will claim attention, among which the improvement of our country by roads and canals, proceeding always with a constitutional sanction, holds a distinguished place. By thus facilitating the intercourse between the States we shall add much to the convenience and comfort of our fellow-citizens, much to the ornament of the country, and, what is of greater importance, we shall shorten distances, and, by making each part more accessible to and dependent on the other, we shall bind the Union more closely together. Nature has done so much for us by intersecting the country with so many great rivers, bays, and lakes, approaching from distant points so near to each other, that the inducement to complete the work seems to be peculiarly strong. A more interesting spectacle was perhaps never seen than is exhibited within the limits of the United States—a territory so vast and advantageously situated, containing objects so grand, so useful, so happily connected in all their parts!

Our manufactures will likewise require the systematic and fostering care of the Government. Possessing as we do all the raw materials, the fruit of our own soil and industry, we ought not to depend in the degree we have done on supplies from other countries. While we are thus dependent the sudden event of war, unsought and unexpected, can not fail to plunge us into the most serious difficulties. It is important, too, that the capital which nourishes our manufactures should be domestic, as its influence in that case instead of exhausting, as it may do in foreign hands, would be felt advantageously on agriculture and every other branch of industry. Equally important is it to provide at home a market for our raw materials, as by extending the competition it will enhance the price and protect the cultivator against the casualties incident to foreign markets.

With the Indian tribes it is our duty to cultivate friendly relations and to act with kindness and liberality in all our transactions. Equally proper is it to persevere in our efforts to extend to them the advantages of civilization.

The great amount of our revenue and the flourishing state of the Treasury are a full proof of the competency of the national resources for any emergency, as they are of the willingness of our fellow-citizens to bear the burdens which the public necessities require. The vast amount of vacant lands, the value of which daily augments, forms an additional resource of great extent and duration. These resources, besides accomplishing every other necessary purpose, put it completely in the power of the United States to discharge the national debt at an early period. Peace is the best time for improvement and preparation of every kind; it is in peace that our commerce flourishes most, that taxes are most easily paid, and that the revenue is most productive.

The Executive is charged officially in the Departments under it with the disbursement of the public money, and is responsible for the faithful application of it to the purposes for which it is raised. The Legislature is the watchful guardian over the public purse. It is its duty to see that the disbursement has been honestly made. To meet the requisite responsibility every facility should be afforded to the Executive to enable it to bring the public agents intrusted with the public money strictly and promptly to account. Nothing should be presumed against them; but if, with the requisite facilities, the public money is suffered to lie long and uselessly in their hands, they will not be the only defaulters, nor will the demoralizing effect be confined to them. It will evince a relaxation and want of tone in the Administration which will be felt by the whole community. I shall do all I can to secure economy and fidelity in this important branch of the Administration, and I doubt not that the Legislature will perform its duty with equal zeal. A thorough examination should be regularly made, and I will promote it.

It is particularly gratifying to me to enter on the discharge of these duties at a time when the United States are blessed with peace. It is a state most consistent with their prosperity and happiness. It will be my sincere desire to preserve it, so far as depends on the Executive, on just principles with all nations, claiming nothing unreasonable of any and rendering to each which is its due.

Equally gratifiying is it to witness the increased harmony of opinion which pervades our Union. Discord does not belong to our system. Union is recommended as well by the free and benign principles of our Government, extending its blessings to every individual, as by the other eminent advantages attending it. The American people have encountered together great dangers and sustained severe trials with success. They constitute one great family with a common interest. Experience has enlightened us on some questions of essential importance to the country. The progress has been slow, dictated by a just reflection and a faithful regard to every interest connected with it. To promote this harmony in accord with the principles of our republican Government and in a manner to give them the most complete effect, and to advance in all other respects the best interests of our Union, will be the object of my constant and zealous exertions.

Never did a government commence under auspices so favorable, nor ever was success so complete. If we look to the history of other nations, ancient or modern, we find no example of a growth so rapid, so gigantic, of a people so prosperous and happy. In contemplating what we have still to perform, the heart of every citizen must expand with joy when he reflects how near our Government has approached to perfection; that in respect to it we have no essential improvement to make; that the great object is to preserve it in the essential principles and features which characterize it, and that that is to be done by preserving the virtue and enlightening the minds of the people; and as a security against foreign dangers to adopt such arrangements as are indispensable to the support of our independence, our rights and liberties. If we persevere in the career in which we have advanced so far and in the path already traced, we can not fail, under the favor of a gracious Providence, to attain the high destiny which seems to await us.

In the Administrations of the illustrious men who have preceded me in this high station, with some of whom I have been connected by the closest ties from early life, examples are presented which will always be found highly instructive and useful to their successors. From these I shall endeavor to derive all the advantages which they may afford. Of my immediate predecessor, under whom so important a portion of this great and successful experiment has been made, I shall be pardoned for expressing my earnest wishes that he may long enjoy in his retirement the affections of a grateful country, the best reward of exalted talents and the most faithful and meritorious services. Relying on the aid to be derived from the other departments of the Government, I enter on the trust to which I have been called by the suffrages of my fellow-citizens with my fervent prayers to the Almighty that He will be graciously pleased to continue to us that protection which He has already so conspicuously displayed in our favor.

REPORT TO CONGRESS ON
JACKSON'S FLORIDA CAMPAIGN
March 25, 1818

*General Andrew Jackson's military campaign in the
Spanish territory of Florida plunged the American
government into a serious dilemma. On the one hand,
Jackson was a highly popular figure in the United
States; on the other hand, his foray into Florida had
resulted in the capture of several Spanish towns and
the execution of two British subjects. In this message
to Congress, Monroe justified the use of American
troops in Spanish territory on the ground that Spain
had failed to restrain Indian attacks as she was
bound to do by treaty.*

To the Senate and the House of Representatives of the United States:

I now lay before Congress all the information in the possession of the
Executive respecting the war with the Seminoles, and the measures which
it has been thought proper to adopt for the safety of our fellow-citizens
on the frontier exposed to their ravages. The inclosed documents show
that the hostilities of this tribe were unprovoked, the offspring of a spirit
long cherished and often manifested toward the United States, and that in
the present instance it was extending itself to other tribes and daily
assuming a more serious aspect. As soon as the nature and object of this
combination were perceived the major-general commanding the Southern
division of the troops of the United States was ordered to the theater of
action, charged with the management of the war and vested with the
powers necessary to give it effect. The season of the year being unfavorable to active operations, and the recesses of the country affording shelter
to these savages in case of retreat, may prevent a prompt termination
of the war; but it may be fairly presumed that it will not be long before
this tribe and its associates receive the punishment which they have pro-
voked and justly merited.

As almost the whole of this tribe inhabits the country within the limits
of Florida, Spain was bound by the treaty of 1795 to restrain them from
committing hostilities against the United States. We have seen with regret that her Government has altogether failed to fulfill this obligation,
nor are we aware that it made any effort to that effect. When we consider her utter inability to check, even in the slightest degree, the movements of this tribe by her very small and incompetent force in Florida,

we are not disposed to ascribe the failure to any other cause. The inability, however, of Spain to maintain her authority over the territory and Indians within her limits, and in consequence to fulfill the treaty, ought not to expose the United States to other and greater injuries. When the authority of Spain ceases to exist there, the United States have a right to pursue their enemy on a principle of self-defense. In this instance the right is more complete and obvious because we shall perform only what Spain was bound to have performed herself. To the high obligations and privileges of this great and sacred right of self-defense will the movement of our troops be strictly confined. Orders have been given to the general in command not to enter Florida unless it be in pursuit of the enemy, and in that case to respect the Spanish authority wherever it is maintained and he will be instructed to withdraw his forces from the Province as soon as he shall have reduced that tribe to order, and secure our fellow-citizens in that quarter by satisfactory arrangements against its unprovoked and savage hostilities in future.

JAMES MONROE.

JAMES MONROE

ANNOUNCEMENT OF TREATY
LIMITING NAVAL FORCES ON GREAT LAKES
April 28, 1818

Exactly one year after this treaty was signed with Great Britain, Monroe made the details known to the American public.

BY THE PRESIDENT OF THE UNITED STATES OF AMERICA.

A PROCLAMATION.

Whereas an arrangement was entered into at the city of Washington in the month of April, A.D. 1817, between Richard Rush, esq., at the time acting as Secretary for the Department of State of the United States for and in behalf of the Government of the United States, and the Right Honorable Charles Bagot, His Britannic Majesty's envoy extraordinary and minister plenipotentiary, for and in behalf of His Britannic Majesty, which arrangement is in the words following, to wit:

The naval force to be maintained upon the American lakes by His Majesty and the Government of the United States shall henceforth be confined to the following vessels on each side; that is—

On Lake Ontario, to one vessel not exceeding 100 tons burden and armed with one 18-pound cannon.

On the upper lakes, to two vessels not exceeding like burden each and armed with like force.

On the waters of Lake Champlain, to one vessel not exceeding like burden and armed with like force.

All other armed vessels on these lakes shall be forthwith dismantled, and no other vessels of war shall be there built or armed.

If either party should hereafter be desirous of annulling this stipulation, and should give notice to that effect to the other party, it shall cease to be binding after the expiration of six months from the date of such notice.

The naval force so to be limited shall be restricted to such service as will in no respect interfere with the proper duties of the armed vessels of the other party.

And whereas the Senate of the United States have approved of the said arrangement and recommended that it should be carried into effect, the same having also received the sanction of His Royal Highness the Prince Regent, acting in the name and on the behalf of His Britannic Majesty:

Now, therefore, I, James Monroe, President of the United States, do by this my proclamation make known and declare that the arrangement aforesaid and every stipulation thereof has been duly entered into, concluded, and confirmed, and is of full force and effect.

Given under my hand, at the city of Washington, this 28th day of April, A. D. 1818, and of the Independence of the United States the forty-second.   JAMES MONROE.

By the President:

John Quincy Adams,
   Secretary of State.

MESSAGE ON THE SLAVE TRADE
December 17, 1819

*In this message to Congress, Monroe discussed legis-
lation which had been passed on March 3, 1819. This
legislation, in brief, provided for the return to Africa
of all Africans illegally found on United States ships
in violation of the anti-slavery acts. More important
perhaps — in view of future events — was the provision
to appoint two agents and send a public ship to
Africa to seek out a "homeland" to which Africans
might be taken. Although a slaveholder himself, Monroe heartily approved of all efforts to return Africans
to Africa. His efforts were recognized in 1824 by the
new African state of Liberia, which named its capital
city "Monrovia" in appreciation of James Monroe.*

To the Senate and House of Representatives of the United States:

Some doubt being entertained respecting the true intent and meaning of
the act of the last session entitled "An act in addition to the acts prohibiting the slave trade," as to the duties of the agents to be appointed on
the coast of Africa, I think it proper to state the interpretation which has
been given of the act and the measures adopted to carry it into effect,
that Congress may, should it be deemed advisable, amend the same before
further proceeding is had under it.

The obligation to instruct the commanders of all our armed vessels to
seize and bring into port all ships or vessels of the United States, where-
soever found, having on board any negro, mulatto, or person of color in
violation of former acts for the suppression of the slave trade, being im-
perative, was executed without delay. No seizures have yet been made,
but as they were contemplated by the law, and might be presumed, it
seemed proper to make the necessary regulations applicable to such seizures
for carrying the several provisions of the act into effect.

It is enjoined on the Executive to cause all negroes, mulattoes, or persons of color who may be taken under the act to be removed to Africa.
It is the obvious import of the law that none of the persons thus taken
should remain within the United States, and no place other than the
coast of Africa being designated, their removal or delivery, whether carried from the United States or landed immediately from the vessels in
which they were taken, was supposed to be confined to that coast. No
settlement or station being specified, the whole coast was thought to be

left open for the selection of a proper place at which the persons thus taken should be delivered. The Executive is authorized to appoint one or more agents residing there to receive such persons, and $100,000 are appropriated for the general purposes of the law.

On due consideration of the several sections of the act, and of its humane policy, it was supposed to be the intention of Congress that all the persons above described who might be taken under it and landed in Africa should be aided in their return to their former homes, or in their establishment at or near the place where landed. Some shelter and food would be necessary for them there as soon as landed, let their subsequent disposition be what it might. Should they be landed without such provision having been previously made, they might perish.

It was supposed, by the authority given to the Executive to appoint agents residing on that coast, that they should provide such shelter and food, and perform the other beneficient and charitable offices contemplated by the act. The coast of Africa having been little explored, and no persons residing there who possessed the requisite qualifications to entitle them to the trust being known to the Executive, to none such could it be committed. It was believed that citizens only who would go hence well instructed in the views of their Government and zealous to give them effect would be competent to these duties, and that it was not the intention of the law to preclude their appointment. It was obvious that the longer these persons should be detained in the United States in the hands of the marshals the greater would be the expense, and that for the same term would the main purpose of the law be suspended. It seemed, therefore, to be incumbent on me to make the necessary arrangements for carrying this act into effect in Africa in time to meet the delivery of any persons who might be taken by the public vessels and landed there under it.

On this view of the policy and sanctions of the law it has been decided to send a public ship to the coast of Africa with two such agents, who will take with them tools and other implements necessary for the purposes above mentioned. To each of these agents a small salary has been allowed—$1,500 to the principal and $1,200 to the other.

All our public agents on the coast of Africa receive salaries for their services, and it was understood that none of our citizens possessing the requisite qualifications would accept these trusts, by which they would be confined to parts the least frequented and civilized, without a reasonable compensation. Such allowance therefore seemed to be indispensable to the execution of the act. It is intended also to subject a portion of the sum appropriated to the order of the principal agent for the special objects above stated, amounting in the whole, including the salaries of the agents for one year, to rather less than one-third of the appropriation. Special instructions will be given to these agents, defining in precise terms their duties in regard to the persons thus delivered to them, the disbursement of the money by the principal agent, and his accountability for the same. They will also have power to select the most suitable place on the coast of Africa at which all persons who may be taken under this act shall be delivered to them, with an express injunction to exercise no power founded on the principle of colonization or other power than that of performing the benevolent offices above recited by the permission and sanction of the existing government under which they may establish themselves. Orders will be given to the commander of the public ship in which they will sail to cruise along the coast to give the more complete effect to the principal object of the act.

JAMES MONROE.

MESSAGE TO CONGRESS
ON SPANISH AFFAIRS IN AMERICA
May 9, 1820

Forming the backdrop to this message were two circumstances which were straining relations between the United States and Spain: first, the reluctance of the Spanish government to ratify the Florida Purchase signed more than one year earlier; second, the growing feeling of independence in the Spanish colonies of South America. In this message, Monroe offered a hint of his famous Monroe Doctrine—delivered some three years later—by announcing the United States' refusal to abandon the right to recognize revolutionary governments in South America.

To the Senate and House of Representatives of the United States:

I communicate to Congress a correspondence which has taken place between the Secretary of State and the envoy extraordinary and minister plenipotentiary of His Catholic Majesty since the message of the 27th March last, respecting the treaty which was concluded between the United States and Spain on the 22d February, 1819.

After the failure of His Catholic Majesty for so long a time to ratify the treaty, it was expected that this minister would have brought with him the ratification, or that he would have been authorized to give an order for the delivery of the territory ceded by it to the United States. It appears, however, that the treaty is still unratified and that the minister has no authority to surrender the territory. The object of his mission has been to make complaints and to demand explanations respecting an imputed system of hostility on the part of citizens of the United States against the subjects and dominions of Spain, and an unfriendly policy in their Government, and to obtain new stipulations against these alleged injuries as the condition on which the treaty should be ratified.

Unexpected as such complaints and such a demand were under existing circumstances, it was thought proper, without compromitting the Government as to the course to be pursued, to meet them promptly and to give the explanations that were desired on every subject with the utmost candor. The result has proved what was sufficiently well known before, that the charge of a systematic hostility being adopted and pursued by citizens of the United States against the dominions and subjects of Spain is utterly destitute of foundation, and that their Government in all its branches has maintained with the utmost rigor that neutrality in the civil war between Spain and the colonies which they were the first to declare. No force has been collected nor incursions made from within the United States against the dominions of Spain, nor have any naval equipments been permitted in favor of either party against the other. Their citizens have been warned of the obligations incident to the neutral condition of their country; their public officers have been instructed to see that the laws were faithfully executed, and severe examples have been made of some who violated them.

In regard to the stipulation proposed as the condition of the ratification of the treaty, that the United States shall abandon the right to recognize the revolutionary colonies in South America, or to form other relations with them when in their judgment it may be just and expedient so to do, it is manifestly so repugnant to the honor and even to the independence of the United States that it has been impossible to discuss it. In making this proposal it is perceived that His Catholic Majesty has entirely misconceived the principles on which this Government has acted in being a party to a negotiation so long protracted for claims so well founded and reasonable, as he likewise has the sacrifices which the United States have made, comparatively, with Spain in the treaty to which it is proposed to annex so extraordinary and improper a condition.

Had the minister of Spain offered an unqualified pledge that the treaty should be ratified by his Sovereign on being made acquainted with the explanations which had been given by this Government, there would have been a strong motive for accepting and submitting it to the Senate for their advice and consent, rather than to resort to other measures for redress, however justifiable and proper; but he gives no such pledge; on the contrary, he declares explicitly that the refusal of this Government to relinquish the right of judging and acting for itself hereafter, according to circumstances, in regard to the Spanish colonies, a right common to all nations, has rendered it impossible for him under his instructions to make such engagement. He thinks that his Sovereign will be induced by his communications to ratify the treaty, but still he leaves him free either to adopt that measure or to decline it. He admits that the other objections are essentially removed and will not in themselves prevent the ratification, provided the difficulty on the third point is surmounted. The result, therefore, is that the treaty is declared to have no obligation whatever; that its ratification is made to depend not on the considerations which led to its adoption and the conditions which it contains, but on a new article unconnected with it, respecting which a new negotiation must be opened, of indefinite duration and doubtful issue.

Under this view of the subject the course to be pursued would appear to be direct and obvious if the affairs of Spain had remained in the state in which they were when this minister sailed. But is is known that an important change has since taken place in the Government of that country which can not fail to be sensibly felt in its intercourse with other nations. The minister of Spain has essentially declared his inability to act in consequence of that change. With him, however, under his present powers nothing could be done. The attitude of the United States must now be assumed on full consideration of what is due to their rights, their interest and honor, without regard to the powers or incidents of the late mission. We may at pleasure occupy the territory which was intended and provided by the late treaty as an indemnity for losses so long since sustained by our citizens; but still, nothing could be settled definitely without a treaty between the two nations. Is this the time to make the pressure? If the United States were governed by views of ambition and aggrandizement, many strong reasons might be given in its favor; but they have no objects of that kind to accomplish, none which are not founded in justice and which can be injured by forbearance. Great hope is entertained that this change will promote the happiness of the Spanish nation. The good order, moderation, and humanity which have characterized the movement are the best guaranties of its success.

The United States would not be justified in their own estimation should they take any step to disturb its harmony. When the Spanish Government is completely organized on the principles of this change, as it is expected it soon will be, there is just ground to presume that our differences with Spain will be speedily and satisfactorily settled.

With these remarks I submit it to the wisdom of Congress whether it will not still be advisable to postpone any decision on this subject until the next session.

JAMES MONROE.

SECOND INAUGURAL ADDRESS
March 5, 1821

Unlike Monroe's first inaugural address, which looked ahead to the policies the President intended to pursue in his first term of office, this address looks back—at what has been achieved during the "Era of Good Feelings." As befits a man who has missed unanimous re-election by only one electoral vote, Monroe was at his most optimistic in this address.

Fellow Citizens:

I shall not attempt to describe the grateful emotions which the new and very distinguished proof of the confidence of my fellow-citizens, evinced by my reelection to this high trust, has excited in my bosom. The approbation which it announces of my conduct in the preceding term affords me a consolation which I shall profoundly feel through life. The general accord with which it has been expressed adds to the great and never-ceasing obligations which it imposes. To merit the continuance of this good opinion, and to carry it with me into my retirement as the solace of advancing years, will be the object of my most zealous and unceasing efforts.

Having no pretensions to the high and commanding claims of my predecessors, whose names are so much more conspicuously identified with our Revolution, and who contributed so preeminently to promote its success, I consider myself rather as the instrument than the cause of the union which has prevailed in the late election. In surmounting, in favor of my humble pretensions, the difficulties which so often produce division in like occurrences, it is obvious that other powerful causes, indicating the great strength and stability of our Union, have essentially contributed to draw you together. That these powerful causes exist, and that they are permanent, is my fixed opinion; that they may produce a like accord in all questions touching, however remotely, the liberty, prosperity, and happiness of our country will always be the object of my most fervent prayers to the Supreme Author of All Good.

In a government which is founded by the people, who possess exclusively the sovereignty, it seems proper that the person who may be placed by their suffrages in this high trust should declare on commencing its duties the principles on which he intends to conduct the Administration. If the person thus elected has served the preceding term, an opportunity is afforded him to review its principal occurrences and to give such further explanation respecting them as in his judgment may be useful to his constituents. The events of one year have influence on those of another, and, in like manner, of a preceding on the succeeding Administration. The movements of a great nation are connected in all their parts. If errors have been committed they ought to be corrected; if the policy is sound it ought to be supported. It is by a thorough knowledge of the whole subject that our fellow-citizens are enabled to judge correctly of the past and to give a proper direction to the future.

Just before the commencement of the last term the United States had concluded a war with a very powerful nation on conditions equal and honorable to both parties. The events of that war are too recent and too deeply impressed on the memory of all to require a development from me. Our commerce had been in a great measure driven from the sea, our Atlantic and inland frontiers were invaded in almost every part; the waste of life along our coast and on some parts of our inland frontiers, to the defense of which our gallant and patriotic citizens were called, was immense, in addition to which not less than $120,000,000 were added at its end to the public debt.

As soon as the war had terminated, the nation, admonished by its events, resolved to place itself in a situation which should be better calculated to prevent the recurrence of a like evil, and, in case it should recur, to mitigate its calamities. With this view, after reducing our land force to the basis of a peace establishment, which has been further modified since, provision was made for the construction of fortifications at proper points through the whole extent of our coast and such an augmentation of our naval force as should be well adapted to both purposes. The laws making this provision were passed in 1815 and 1816, and it has been since the constant effort of the Executive to carry them into effect.

The advantage of these fortifications and of an augmented naval force in the extent contemplated, in a point of economy, has been fully illustrated by a report of the Board of Engineers and Naval Commissioners lately communicated to Congress, by which it appears that in an invasion by 20,000 men, with a correspondent naval force, in a campaign of six months only, the whole expense of the construction of the works should be defrayed by the difference in the sum necessary to maintain the force which would be adequate to our defense with the aid of those works and that which would be incurred without them. The reason of this difference is obvious. If fortifications are judiciously placed on our great inlets, as distant from our cities as circumstances will permit, they will form the only points of attack, and the enemy will be detained there by a small regular force a sufficient time to enable our militia to collect and repair to that on which the attack is made. A force adequate to the enemy, collected at that single point, with suitable preparation for such others as might be menaced, is all that would be requisite. But if there were no fortifications, then the enemy might go where he pleased, and, changing his position and sailing from place to place, our force must be called out and spread in vast numbers along the whole coast and on both sides of every bay and river as high up in each as it might be navigable for ships of war. By these fortifications, supported by our Navy, to which they would afford like support, we should present to other powers an armed front from St. Croix to the Sabine, which would protect in the event of war our whole coast and interior from invasion; and even in the wars of other powers, in which we were neutral, they would be found eminently useful, as, by keeping their public ships at a distance from our cities, peace and order in them would be preserved and the Government be protected from insult.

It need scarcely be remarked that these measures have not been resorted to in a spirit of hostility to other powers. Such a disposition does not exist toward any power. Peace and good will have been, and will hereafter be, cultivated with all, and by the most faithful regard to justice. They have been dictated by a love of peace, of economy, and an earnest desire to save the lives of our fellow-citizens from that destruction and our country from that devastation which are inseparable from war when it finds us unprepared for it. It is believed, and experience has shown, that such a preparation is the best expedient that can be resorted to to prevent war. I add with much pleasure that considerable progress has already been made in these measures of defense, and that they will be completed in a few years, considering the great extent and importance of the object, if the plan be zealously and steadily persevered in.

The conduct of the Government in what relates to foreign powers is always an object of the highest importance to the nation. Its agriculture, commerce, manufactures, fisheries, revenue, in short, its peace, may all be affected by it. Attention is therefore due to this subject.

At the period adverted to the powers of Europe, after having been engaged in long and destructive wars with each other, had concluded a peace, which happily still exists. Our peace with the power with whom we had been engaged had also been concluded. The war between Spain and the colonies in South America, which had commenced many years before, was then the only conflict that remained unsettled. This being a contest between different parts of the same community, in which other powers had not interefered, was not affected by their accommodations.

This contest was considered at an early stage by my predecessor a civil war in which the parties were entitled to equal rights in our ports. This decision, the first made by any power, being formed on great consideration of the comparative strength and resources of the parties, the length of time, and successful opposition made by the colonies, and of all other circumstances on which it ought to depend, was in strict accord with the law of nations. Congress has invariably acted on this principle, having made no change in our relations with either party. Our attitude has therefore been that of neutrality between them, which has been maintained by the Government with the strictest impartiality. No aid has been afforded to either, nor has any privilege been enjoyed by the one which has not been equally open to the other party, and every exertion has been made in its power to enforce the execution of the laws prohibiting illegal equipments with equal rigor against both.

By this equality between the parties their public vessels have been received in our ports on the same footing; they have enjoyed an equal right to purchase and export arms, munitions of war, and every other supply, the exportation of all articles whatever being permitted under laws which were passed long before the commencement of the contest; our citizens have traded equally with both, and their commerce with each has been alike protected by the Government.

Respecting the attitude which it may be proper for the United States to maintain hereafter between the parties, I have no hesitation in stating it as my opinion that the neutrality heretofore observed should still be adhered to. From the change in the Government of Spain and the negotiation now depending, invited by the Cortes and accepted by the colonies, it may be presumed, that their differences will be settled on the terms proposed by the colonies. Should the war be continued, the United States, regarding its occurrences, will always have it in their power to adopt such measures repsecting it as their honor and interest may require.

Shortly after the general peace a band of adventurers took advantage of this conflict and of the facility, which it afforded to establish a system of buccaneering in the neighboring seas, to the great annoyance of the commerce of the United States, and, as was represented, of that of other powers. Of this spirit and of its injurious bearing on the United States strong proofs were afforded by the establishment at Amelia Island, and the purposes to which it was made instrumental by this band in 1817. and by the occurrences which took place in other parts of Florida in 1818, the details of which in both instances are too well known to require to be now recited. I am satisfied had a less decisive course been adopted that the worst consequences would have resulted from it. We have been that these checks, decisive as they were, were not sufficient to crush that piratical spirit. Many culprits brought within our limits have been condemned to suffer death, the punishment due to that atrocious crime. The decisions of upright and enlightened tribunals fall equally on all whose crimes subject them, by a fair interpretation of the law, to its censure. It belongs to the Executive not to suffer the executions under these decisions to transcend the great purpose for which punishment in necessary. The full benefit of example being secured, policy as well as humanity equally forbids that they should be carried further. I have acted on this principle, pardoning those who appear to have been led astray by ignorance of the criminality of the acts they had committed, and suffering the law to take effect on those only in whose favor no extenuating circumstances could be urged.

Great confidence is entertained that the late treaty with Spain, which has been ratified by both the parties, and the ratifications whereof have been exchanged, has placed the relations of the two countries on a basis of permanent friendship. The provision made by it for such of our citizens as have claims on Spain of the character described, will, it is presumed, be very satisfactory to them, and the boundary which is established between the territories of the parties westward of the Mississippi, heretofore in dispute has, it is thought, been settled on conditions just and advantageous to both. But to the acquisition of Florida too much importance can not be attached. It secures to the United States a territory important in itself, and whose importance is much increased by its bearing on many of the highest interests of the Union. It opens to several of the neighboring States a free passage to the ocean, through the Province ceded, by several rivers, having their sources high up within their limits. It secures us against all future annoyance from powerful Indian tribes. It gives us several excellent harbors in the Gulf of Mexico for ships of war of the largest size. It covers by its position in the Gulf the Mississippi and other great waters within our extended limits, and thereby enables the United States to afford complete protection to the vast and very valuable productions of our whole Western country, which find a market through those streams.

By a treaty with the British Government, bearing date on the 20th of October, 1818, the convention regulating the commerce between the United States and Great Britain, concluded on the 3d of July, 1815, which was about expiring, was revived and continued for the term of ten years from the time of its expiration. By that treaty, also, the differences which had arisen under the treaty of Ghent respecting the right claimed by the United States for their citizens to take and cure fish on the coast of His Britannic Majesty's dominions in America, with other differences on important interests, were adjusted to the satisfaction of both parties. No agreement has yet been entered into respecting the commerce between the United States and the British dominions in the West Indies and on this continent. The restraints imposed on that commerce by Great Britain, and reciprocated by the United States on a principle of defense, continue still in force.

The negotiations with France for the regulation of the commercial relations between the two countries, which in the course of the last summer had been commenced at Paris, has since been transferred to this city, and will be pursued on the part of the United States in the spirit of conciliation, and with an earnest desire that it may terminate in an arrangement satisfactory to both parties.

Our relations with the Barbary Powers are preserved in the same state and by the same means that were employed when I came into this office.

As early as 1801 it was found necessary to send a squadron into the Mediterranean for the protection of our commerce, and no period has intervened, a short term accepted, when it was thought advisable to withdraw it. The great interests which the United States have in the Pacific, in commerce and in the fisheries, have also made it necessary to maintain a naval force there. In dispensing of this force in both instances the most effectual measures in our powers have been taken, without interfering with its other duties, for the suppression of the slave trade and of piracy in the neighboring seas.

The situation of the United States in regard to their resources, the extent of their revenue, and the facility with which it is raised affords a most gratifying spectacle. The payment of nearly $67,000,000 of the public debt, with the great progress made in measures of defense and in other improvements of various kinds since the late war, are conclusive proofs of this extraordinary prosperity, especially when it is recollected that these expenditures have been defrayed without a burthen on the people, the direct tax and excise having been repealed soon after the conclusion of the late war, and the revenue applied to these great objects having been raised in a manner not to be felt. Our great resources therefore remain untouched for any purpose which may affect the vital interests of the nation. For all such purposes they are inexhaustible. They are more especially to be found in the virtue, patriotism, and intelligence of our fellow-citizens, and in the devotion with which they would yield up by any just measure of taxation all their property in support of the rights and honor of their country.

Under the present depression of prices, affecting all the productions of the country and every branch of industry, proceeding from causes explained on a former occasion, the revenue has considerably diminished, the effect of which has been to compel Congress either to abandon these great measures of defense or to resort to loans or internal taxes to supply the deficiency. On the presumption that this depression and the deficiency in the revenue arising from it would be temporary, loans were authorized for the demands of the last and present year. Anxious to relieve my fellow-citizens in 1817 from every burthen which could be dispensed with, and the state of the Treasury permitting it, I recommended the repeal of the internal taxes, knowing that such relief was then peculiarly necessary in consequence of the great exertions made in the late war. I made that recommendation under a pledge that should the public exigencies require a recurrence to them at any time while I remained in this trust, I would with equal promptidue perform the duty which would then be alike incumbent on me. By the experiment now making it will be seen by the next session of Congress whether the revenue shall have been so augmented as to be adequate to all these necessary purposes. Should the deficiency still continue, and especially should it be probable that it would be permanent, the course to be pursued appears to me to be obvious. I am satisfied that under certain circumstances loans may be resorted to with great advantage. I am equally well satisfied, as a general rule, that the demands of the current year, especially in time of peace, should be provided for by the revenue of that year.

I have never dreaded, nor have I ever shunned, in any situation in which I have been placed making appeals to the virtue and patriotism of my fellow-citizens, well knowing that they could never be made in vain, especially in times of great emergency or for purposes of high national importance. Independently of the exigency of the case, many considerations of great weight urge a policy having in view a provision of revenue to meet to a certain extent the demands of the nation, without relying altogether on the precarious resource of foreign commerce. I am satisfied that internal duties and excises, with corresponding imposts on foreign articles of the same kind, would, without imposing any serious burdens on the people, enhance the price of produce, promote our manufactures, and augment the revenue, at the same time that they made it more secure and permanent.

The case of the Indian tribes within our limits has long been an essential part of our system, but, unfortunately, it has not been executed in a manner to accomplish all the objects intended by it. We have treated them as independent nations, without their having any substantial pretensions to that rank. The distinction has flattered their pride, retarded their improvement, and in many instances paved the way to their destruction. The progress of our settlements westward, supported as they are by a dense population, has constantly driven them back, with almost the total sacrifice of the lands which they have been compelled to abandon. They have claims on the magnanimity and, I may add, on the justice of this nation which we must all feel. We should become their real benefactors; we should perform the office of their Great Father, the endearing title which they emphatically give to the Chief Magistrate of our Union. Their sovereignty over vast territories should cease, in lieu of which the right of soil should be secured to each individual and his posterity in competent portions; and for the territory thus ceded by each tribe some reasonable equivalent should be granted, to be vested in permanent funds for the support of civil government over them and for the education of their children, for their instruction in the arts of husbandry, and to provide sustenance for them until they could provide it for themselves. My earnest hope is that Congress will digest some plan, founded on these principles, with such improvements as their wisdom may suggest, and carry it into effect as soon as it may be practicable.

Europe is again unsettled and the prospect of war increasing. Should the flame light up in any quarter, how far it may extend it is impossible to foresee. It is our peculiar felicity to be altogether unconnected with the causes which produce this menacing aspect elsewhere. With every power we are in perfect amity, and it is our interest to remain so if it be practicable on just conditions. I see no reasonable cause to apprehend variance with any power, unless it proceed from a violation of our maritime rights. In these contests, should they occur, and to whatever extent they may be carried, we shall be neutral; but as a neutral power we have rights which it is our duty to maintain. For like injuries it will be incumbent on us to seek redress in a spirit of amity, in full confidence that, injuring none, none would knowingly injure us. For more imminent dangers we should be prepared, and it should always be recollected that such preparation adapted to the circumstances and sanctioned by the judgment and wishes of our constituents can not fail to have a good effect in averting dangers of every kind. We should recollect also that the season of peace is best adapted to these preparations.

If we turn our attention, fellow-citizens, more immediately to the internal concerns of our country, and more especially to those on which its future welfare depends, we have every reason to anticipate the happiest results. It is now rather more than forty-four years since we declared our independence, and thirty-seven since it was acknowledged. The talents and virtues which were displayed in that great struggle were a sure presage of all that has since followed. A people who were able to surmount in their infant state such great perils would be more competent as they rose into manhood to repel any which they might meet in their progress. Their physical strength would be more adequate to foreign danger, and the practice of self-government, aided by the light of experience, could not fail to produce an effect equally salutary on all those questions connected with the internal organization. These favorable anticipations have been realized.

In our whole system, national and State, we have shunned all the defects which unceasingly preyed on the vitals and destroyed the ancient Republics. In them there were distinct orders, a nobility and a people, or the people governed in one assembly. Thus, in the one instance there was a perpetual conflict between the orders in society for the ascendency, in which the victory of either terminated in the overthrow of the government and the ruin of the state; in the other, in which the people governed in a body, and whose dominions seldom exceeded the dimensions of a county in one of our States, a tumultous and disorderly movement permitted only a transitory existence. In this great nation there is but one order, that of the people, whose power, by a peculiarly happy improvement of the representative principle, is transferred from them, without impairing in the slightest degree their sovereignty, to bodies of their own creation, and to persons elected by themselves, in the full extent necessary for all the purposes of free, enlightened, and efficient government. The whole system is elective, the complete sovereignty being in the people, and every officer in every department deriving his authority from and being responsible to them for his conduct.

Our career has corresponded with this great outline. Perfection in our organization could not have been expected in the outset either in the National or State Governments or in tracing the line between their respective powers. But no serious conflict has arisen, nor any contest but such as are managed by argument and by a fair appeal to the good sense of the people, and many of the defects which experience had clearly demonstrated in both Governments have been remedied. By steadily pursuing this course in this spirit there is every reason to believe that our system will soon attain the highest degree of perfection of which human institutions are capable, and that the movements in all its branches will exhibit such a degree of order and harmony as to command the admiration and respect of the civilized world.

Our physical attainments have not been less eminent. Twenty-five years ago the river Mississippi was shut up and our Western brethren had no outlet for their commerce. What has been the progress since that time? The river has not only become the property of the United States from its source to the ocean, with all its tributary streams (with the exception of the upper part of the Red River only), but Louisiana, with a fair and liberal boundary on the western side and the Floridas on the eastern, have been ceded to us. The United States now enjoy the complete and uninterrupted sovereignty over the whole territory from St. Croix to the Sabine. New States, settled from among ourselves in this and in other parts, have been admitted into our Union in equal participation in the national sovereignty with the original States. Our population has augmented in an astonishing degree and extended in every direction. We now, fellow-citizens, comprise within our limits the dimensions and faculties of a great power under a Government possessing all the energies of any government ever known to the Old World, with an utter incapacity to oppress the people.

Entering with these views the office which I have just solemnly sworn to execute with fidelity and to the utmost of my ability, I derive great satisfaction from a knowledge that I shall be assisted in the several Departments by the very enlightened and upright citizens from whom I have received so much aid in the preceding term. With full confidence in the continuance of that candor and generous indulgence from my fellow-citizens at large which I have heretofore experienced, and with a firm reliance on the protection of Almighty God, I shall forthwith commence the duties of the high trust to which you have called me.

JAMES MONROE

MESSAGE TO CONGRESS
ON SOUTH AMERICAN REPUBLICS
March 8, 1822

This message represents one further "escalation" in United States sympathy for the South American republics, which were struggling for independence from Spain. Monroe not only recommended recognition of the independent South American governments, but also asked for an appropriation for ministers to South America. He reviewed at great length the history of the revolutions and the declarations of independence by Mexico, Chile, Peru, Argentina and Colombia, and stated that since Spain, after so many years of attempt, had failed to subdue them, they were actually in a state of independence and deserved to be recognized.

To the Senate and House of Representatives of the United States:

In transmitting to the House of Representatives the documents called for by the resolution of that House of the 30th January, I consider it my duty to invite the attention of Congress to a very important subject, and to communicate the sentiments of the Executive on it, that, should Congress entertain similar sentiments, there may be such cooperation between the two departments of the Government as their respective rights and duties may require.

The revolutionary movement in the Spanish Provinces in this hemisphere attracted the attention and excited the sympathy of our fellow-citizens from its commencement. This feeling was natural and honorable to them, from causes which need not be communicated to you. It has been gratifying to all to see the general acquiescence which has been manifested in the policy which the constituted authorities have deemed it proper to pursue in regard to this contest. As soon as the movement assumed such a steady and consistent form as to make the success of the Provinces probable, the rights to which they were entitled by the law of nations as equal parties to a civil war were extended to them. Each party was permitted to enter our ports with its public and private ships, and to take from them every article which was the subject of commerce with other nations. Our citizens, also, have carried on commerce with both parties, and the Government has protected it with each in articles not contraband of war. Through the whole of this contest the United States have remained neutral, and have fulfilled with the utmost impartiality all the obligations incident to that character.

This contest has now reached such a stage and been attended with such decisive success on the part of the Provinces that it merits the most profound consideration whether their right to the rank of independent nations, with all the advantages incident to it in their intercourse with the United States, is not complete. Buenos Ayres assumed that rank by a formal declaration in 1816, and has enjoyed it since 1810 free from invasion by the parent country. The Provinces composing the Republic of Colombia, after having separately declared their independence, were united by a fundamental law of the 17th of December, 1819. A strong Spanish force occupied at that time certain parts of the territory within their limits and waged a destructive war. That force has since been repeatedly defeated, and the whole of it either made prisoners or destroyed or expelled from the country, with the exception of an inconsiderable portion only, which is blockaded in two fortresses. The Provinces on the Pacific have likewise been very successful. Chili declared independence in 1818, and has since enjoyed it undisturbed; and of late, by the assistance of Chili and Buenos Ayres, the revolution has extended to Peru. Of the movement in Mexico our information is less authentic, but it is, nevertheless, distinctly understood that the new Government has declared its independence, and that there is now no opposition to it there nor a force to make any. For the last three years the Government of Spain has not sent a single corps of troops to any part of that country, nor is there any reason to believe it will send any in future. Thus it is manifest that all those Provinces are not only in the full enjoyment of their independence, but, considering the state of the war and other circumstances, that there is not the most remote prospect of their being deprived of it.

When the result of such a contest is manifestly settled, the new governments have a claim to recognition by other powers which ought not to be resisted. Civil wars too often excite feelings which the parties can not control. The opinion entertained by other powers as to the result may assuage those feelings and promote an accommodation between them useful and honorable to both. The delay which has been observed in making a decision on this important subject will, it is presumed, have afforded an unequivocal proof to Spain, as it must have done to other powers, of the high respect entertained by the United States for her rights and of their determination not to interfere with them. The Provinces belonging to this hemisphere are our neighbors, and have successively, as each portion of the country acquired its independence, pressed their recognition by an appeal to facts not to be contested, and which they thought gave them a just title to it. To motives of interest this government has invariably disclaimed all pretension, being resolved to take no part in the controversy or other measure in regard to it which should not merit the sanction of the civilized world. To other claims a just sensibility has been always felt and frankly acknowledged, but they in themselves could never become an adequate cause of action. It was incumbent on this Government to look to every important fact and circumstance on which a sound opinion could be formed, which has been done. When we regard, then, the great length of time which this war has been prosecuted, the complete success which has attended it in favor of the Provinces, the present condition of the parties, and the utter inability of Spain to produce any change in it, we are compelled to conclude that its fate is settled, and that the Provinces which have declared their independence and are in the enjoyment of it ought to be recognized.

Of the views of the Spanish Government on this subject no particular information has been recently received. It may be presumed that the successful progress of the revolution through such a long series of years, gaining strength and extending annually in every direction, and embracing by the late important events, with little exception, all the dominions of Spain south of the United States on this continent, placing thereby the complete sovereignty over the whole in the hands of the people, will reconcile the parent country to an accommodation with them on the basis of their unqualified independence. Nor has any authentic information been recently received of the disposition of other powers respecting it. A sincere desire has been cherished to act in concert with them in the proposed recognition, of which several were some time past duly apprised; but it was understood that they were not prepared for it. The immense space between those powers, even those which border on the Atlantic, and these Provinces makes the movement an affair of less interest and excitement to them than to us. It is probable, therefore, that they have been less attentive to its progress than we have been. It may be presumed, however, that the late events will dispel all doubt of the result.

In proposing this measure it is not contemplated to change thereby in the slightest manner our friendly relations with either of the parties, but to observe in all respects, as heretofore, should the war be continued, the most perfect neutrality between them. Of this friendly disposition an assurance will be given to the Government of Spain, to whom it is presumed it will be, as it ought to be, satisfactory. The measure is proposed under a thorough conviction that it is in strict accord with the law of nations, that it is just and right as to the parties, and that the United States owe it to their station and character in the world, as well as to their essential interests, to adopt it. Should Congress concur in the view herein presented, they will doubtless see the propriety of making the necessary appropriations for carrying it into effect.

JAMES MONROE.

JAMES MONROE

PRESIDENTIAL VETO
May 4, 1822

By this date, the Cumberland Road had already assumed a great importance in American history. Originally planned to run from Cumberland, Md. to St. Louis, it had been started in 1811 and had been completed as far as Wheeling, W. Va., when the financial panic of 1819 temporarily suspended activity. The West—championed by Henry Clay—saw in the Road the beginning of trade and, in effect, the solution of its difficulties. On April 29, 1822, Congress passed a bill appropriating $9,000 for the repair of the Cumberland Road. It was vetoed by Monroe in this message to Congress. His main reason: since violators of regulations would have to be dealt with on a Federal level, the measure would be an infringement on the police powers of the states. Simultaneous with this bill, Monroe delivered a lengthy message to Congress, urging a Constitutional Amendment to clear up what he believed was a conflict between the Constitution and Congressional authority over public works.

To the House of Representatives:

Having duly considered the bill entitled "An act for the preservation and repair of the Cumberland road," it is with deep regret, approving as I do the policy, that I am compelled to object to its passage and to return the bill to the House of Representatives, in which it originated, under a conviction that Congress do not possess the power under the Constitution to pass such a law.

A power to establish turnpikes with gates and tolls, and to enforce the collection of tolls by penalties, implies a power to adopt and execute a complete system of internal improvement. A right to impose duties to be paid by all persons passing a certain road, and on horses and carriages, as is done by this bill, involves the right to take the land from the proprietor on a valuation and to pass laws for the protection of the road from injuries, and if it exist as to one road it exists as to any other, and to as many roads as Congress may think proper to establish. A right to legislate for one of these purposes is a right to legislate for the others. It is a complete right of jurisdiction and sovereignty for all the purposes of internal improvement, and not merely the right of applying money under the power vested in Congress to make appropriations, under which power, with the consent of the States through which this road passes, the work was originally commenced, and has been so far executed. I am of opinion that Congress do not possess this power; that the States individually can not grant it, for although they may assent to the appropriation of money within their limits for such purposes, they can grant no power of jurisdiction or sovereignty by special compacts with the United States. This power can be granted only by an amendment to the Constitution and in the mode prescribed by it.

If the power exist, it must be either because it has been specifically granted to the United States or that it is incidental to some power which has been specifically granted. If we examine the specific grants of power we do not find it among them, nor is it incidental to any power which has been specifically granted.

It has never been contended that the power was specifically granted. It is claimed only as being incidental to some one or more of the powers which are specifically granted. The following are the powers from which it is said to be derived:

First, from the right to establish post-offices and post-roads; second, from the right to declare war; third, to regulate commerce; fourth, to pay the debts and provide for the common defense and general welfare; fifth, from the power to make all laws necessary and proper for carrying into execution all the powers vested by the Contitution in the Government of the United States or in any department or officer thereof; sixth and lastly, from the power to dispose of and make all needful rules and regulations respecting the territory and other property of the United States.

According to my judgment it can not be derived from either of those powers, nor from all of them united, and in consequence it does not exist.

Having stated my objections to the bill, I should now cheerfully communicate at large the reasons on which they are founded if I had time to reduce them to such form as to include them in this paper. The advanced stage of the session renders that impossible. Having at the commencement of my service in this high trust considered it a duty to express the opinion that the United States do not possess the power in question, and to suggest for the consideration of Congress the propriety of recommending to the States an amendment to the Constitution to vest the power in the United States, my attention has been often drawn to the subject since, in consequence whereof I have occasionally committed my sentiments to paper respecting it. The form which this exposition has assumed is not such as I should have given it had it been intended for Congress, nor is it concluded. Nevertheless, as it contains my views on this subject, being one which I deem of very high importance, and which in many of its bearings has now become peculiarly urgent, I will communicate it to Congress, if in my power, in the course of the day, or certainly on Monday next.

JAMES MONROE.

THE MONROE DOCTRINE
December 2, 1823

*This document is without doubt the most famous
public statement ever delivered by James Monroe.
It is quite possibly the most renowned doctrine ever
promulgated by an American statesman—anywhere,
at any time. Contrary to popular opinion, however,
it was not delivered as a separate, isolated statement
of American policy; rather, it was contained in Monroe's Seventh Annual Message to Congress. In essence,
the Doctrine consists of two basic points: that the
two American continents are no longer to be considered subjects for future European colonization;
and that any attempt by European powers to extend
their influence into the Western Hemisphere would
be considered dangerous to the United States' peace
and safety.*

Fellow-Citizens of the Senate and House of Representatives:

Many important subjects will claim your attention during the present
session, of which I shall endeavor to give, in aid of your deliberations, a
just idea in this communication. I undertake this duty with diffidence,
from the vast extent of the interests on which I have to treat and of their
great importance to every portion of our Union. I enter on it with zeal
from a thorough conviction that there never was a period since the establishment of our Revolution when, regarding the condition of the civilized world and its bearing on us, there was greater necessity for devotion
in the public servants to their respective duties, or for virtue, patriotism,
and union in our constituents.

Meeting in you a new Congress, I deem it proper to present this view
of public affairs in greater detail than might otherwise be necessary. I
do it, however, with peculiar satisfaction, from a knowledge that in this
respect I shall comply more fully with the sound principles of our Government. The people being with us exclusively the sovereign, it is indispensable that full information be laid before them on all important subjects,
to enable them to exercise that high power with complete effect. If kept
in the dark, they must be incompetent to it. We are all liable to error,
and those who are engaged in the management of public affairs are more
subject to excitement and to be led astray by their particular interests
and passions than the great body of our constituents, who, living at home
in the pursuit of their ordinary avocations, are calm but deeply interested

spectators of events and of the conduct of those who are parties to them. To the people every department of the Government and every individual in each are responsible, and the more full their information the better they can judge of the wisdom of the policy pursued and of the conduct of each in regard to it. From their dispassionate judgment much aid may always be obtained, while their approbation will form the greatest incentive and most gratifying reward for virtuous actions, and the dread of their censure the best security against the abuse of their confidence. Their interests in all vital questions are the same, and the bond, by sentiment as well as by interest, will be proportionably strengthened as they are better informed of the real state of public affairs, especially in difficult conjunctures. It is by such knowledge that local prejudices and jealousies are surmounted, and that a national policy, extending its fostering care and protection to all the great interests of our Union, is formed and steadily adhered to.

A precise knowledge of our relations with foreign powers as respects our negotiations and transactions with each is thought to be particularly necessary. Equally necessary is it that we should form a just estimate of our resources, revenue, and progress in every kind of improvement connected with the national prosperity and public defense. It is by rendering justice to other nations that we may expect it from them. It is by our ability to resent injuries and redress wrongs that we may avoid them.

The commissioners under the fifth article of the treaty of Ghent, having disagreed in their opinions respecting that portion of the boundary between the Territories of the United States and of Great Britain the establishment of which had been submitted to them, have made their respective reports in compliance with that article, that the same might be referred to the decision of a friendly power. It being manifest, however, that it would be difficult, if not impossible, for any power to perform that office without great delay and much inconvenience to itself, a proposal has been made by this Government, and acceded to by that of Great Britain, to endeavor to establish that boundary by amicable negotiation. It appearing from long experience that no satisfactory arrangement could be formed of the commercial intercourse between the United States and the British colonies in this hemisphere by legislative acts while each party pursued its own course without agreement or concert with the other, a proposal has been made to the British Government to regulate this commerce by treaty, as it has been to arrange in like manner the just claim of the citizens of the United States inhabiting the States and Territories bordering on the lakes and rivers which empty into the St. Lawrence to the navigation of that river to the ocean. For these and other objects of high importance to the interests of both parties a negotiation has been opened with the British Government which it is hoped will have a satisfactory result.

The commissioners under the sixth and seventh articles of the treaty of Ghent having successfully closed their labors in relation to the sixth, have proceeded to the discharge of those relating to the seventh. Their progress in the extensive survey required for the performance of their duties justifies the presumption that it will be completed in the ensuing year.

The negotiations which had been long depending with the French Government on several important subjects, and particularly for a just indemnity for losses sustained in the late wars by the citizens of the United States under unjustifiable seizures and confiscations of their property, has not as yet had the desired effect. As this claim rests on the same principle with others which have been admitted by the French Government, it is not perceived on what just ground it can be rejected. A minister will be immediately appointed to proceed to France and resume the negotiation on this and other subjects which may arise between the two nations.

At the proposal of the Russian Imperial Government, made through the minister of the Emperor residing here, a full power and instructions have been transmitted to the minister of the United States at St. Petersburg to arrange by amicable negotiation the respective rights and interests of the two nations on the northwest coast of this continent. A similar proposal had been made by His Imperial Majesty to the Government of Great Britain, which has likewise been acceded to. The Government of the United States has been desirous by this friendly proceeding of manifesting the great value which they have invariably attached to the friendship of the Emperor and their solicitude to cultivate the best understanding with his Government. In the discussions to which this interest has given rise and in the arrangements by which they may terminate the occasion has been judged proper for asserting, as a principle in which the rights and interests of the United States are involved, that the American continents, by the free and independent condition which they have assumed and maintain, are henceforth not to be considered as subjects for future colonization by any European powers.

Since the close of the last session of Congress the commissioners and arbitrators for ascertaining and determining the amount of indemnification which may be due to citizens of the United States under the decision of His Imperial Majesty the Emperor of Russia, in conformity to the convention concluded at St. Petersburg on the 12th of July, 1822, have assembled in this city, and organized themselves as a board for the performance of the duties assigned to them by that treaty. The commission constituted under the eleventh article of the treaty of the 22d of February, 1819, between the United States and Spain is also in session here, and as the term of three years limited by the treaty for the execution of the trust will expire before the period of the next regular ·meeting of Congress, the attention of the Legislature will be drawn to the measures which may be necessary to accomplish the objects for which the commission was instituted.

In compliance with a resolution of the House of Representatives adopted at their last session, instructions have been given to all the ministers of the United States accredited to the powers of Europe and America to propose the proscription of the African slave trade by classing it under the denomination, and inflicting on its perpetrators the punishment, of piracy. Should this proposal be acceded to, it is not doubted that this odious and criminal practice will be promptly and entirely suppressed. It is earnestly hoped that it will be acceded to, from the firm belief that it is the most effectual expedient that can be adopted for the purpose.

At the commencement of the recent war between France and Spain it was declared by the French Government that it would grant no commissions to privateers, and that neither the commerce of Spain herself nor of neutral nations should be molested by the naval force of France, except in the breach of a lawful blockade. This declaration, which appears to have been faithfully carried into effect, concurring with principles proclaimed and cherished by the United States from the first establishment of their independence, suggested the hope that the time had arrived when the proposal for adopting it as a permanent and invariable rule in all future maritime wars might meet the favorable consideration of the great European powers. Instructions have accordingly been given to our ministers with France, Russia, and Great Britain to make those proposals to their respective Governments, and when the friends of humanity reflect on the essential amelioration to the condition of the human race which would result from the abolition of private war on the sea and on the great facility by which it might be accomplished, requiring only the consent of a few sovereigns, an earnest hope is indulged that theese overtures will meet with an attention animated by the spirit in which they were made, and that they will ultimately be successful.

The ministers who were appointed to the Republics of Colombia and Buenos Ayres during the last session of Congress proceeded shortly afterwards to their destinations. Of their arrival there official intelligence has not yet been received. The minister appointed to the Republic of Chile will sail in a few days. An early appointment will also be made to Mexico. A minister has been received from Colombia, and the other Governments have been informed that ministers, or diplomatic agents of inferior grade, would be received from each, accordingly as they might prefer the one or the other.

The minister appointed to Spain proceeded soon after his appointment for Cadiz, the residence of the Sovereign to whom he was accredited. In approaching that port the frigate which conveyed him was warned off by the commander of the French squadron by which it was blockaded and not permitted to enter, although apprised by the captain of the frigate of the public character of the person whom he had on board, the landing of whom was the sole object of his proposed entry. This act, being considered an infringement of the rights of ambassadors and of nations, will form a just cause of complaint to the Government of France against the officer by whom it was committed.

The actual condition of the public finances more than realizes the favorable anticipations that were entertained of it at the opening of the last session of Congress. On the 1st of January there was a balance in the Treasury of $4,237,427.55. From that time to the 30th September the receipts amounted to upward of $16,100,000, and the expenditures to $11,400,000. During the fourth quarter of the year it is estimated that the receipts will at least equal the expenditures, and that there will remain in the Treasury on the 1st day of January next a surplus of nearly $9,000,000.

On the 1st of January, 1825, a large amount of the war debt and a part of the Revolutionary debt become redeemable. Additional portions of the former will continue to become redeemable annually until the year 1835. It is believed, however, that if the United States remain at peace the whole of that debt may be redeemed by the ordinary revenue of those years during that period under the provision of the act of March 3, 1817, creating the sinking fund, and in that case the only part of the debt that will remain after the year 1835 will be the $7,000,000 of 5 per cent stock subscribed to the Bank of the United States, and the 3 per cent Revolutionary debt, amounting to $13,296,099.06, both of which are redeemable at the pleasure of the Government.

The state of the Army in its organization and discipline has been gradually improving for several years, and has now attained a high degree of perfection. The military disbursements have been regularly made and the accounts regularly and promptly rendered for settlement. The supplies of various descriptions have been of good quality, and regularly issued at all of the posts. A system of economy and accountability has been introduced into every branch of the service which admits of little additional improvement. This desirable state has been attained by the act reorganizing the staff of the Army, passed on the 14th of April, 1818.

The moneys appropriated for fortifications have been regularly and economically applied, and all the works advanced as rapidly as the amount appropriated would admit. Three important works will be completed in the course of this year—that is, Fort Washington, Fort Delaware, and the fort at the Rigolets, in Louisiana.

The Board of Engineers and the Topographical Corps have been in constant and active service in surveying the coast and projecting the works necessary for its defense.

The Military Academy has attained a degree of perfection in its discipline and instruction equal, as is believed, to any institution of its kind in any country.

The money appropriated for the use of the Ordnance Department has been regularly and economically applied. The fabrication of arms at the national armories and by contract with the Department has been gradually improving in quality and cheapness. It is believed that their quality is now such as to admit of but little improvement.

The completion of the fortifications renders it necessary that there should be a suitable appropriation for the purpose of fabricating the cannon and carriages necessary for those works.

Under the appropriation of $5,000 for exploring the Western waters for the location of a site for a Western armory, a commission was constituted consisting of Colonel McRee, Colonel Lee, and Captain Talcott, who have been engaged in exploring the country. They have not yet reported the result of their labors, but it is believed that they will be prepared to do it at any early part of the session of Congress.

During the month of June last General Ashley and his party, who were trading under a license from the Government, were attacked by the Ricarees while peaceably trading with the Indians at their request. Several of the party were killed and wounded and their property taken or destroyed.

Colonel Leavenworth, who commanded Fort Atkinson, at the Council Bluffs, the most western post, apprehending that the hostile spirit of the Ricarees would extend to other tribes in that quarter, and that thereby the lives of the traders on the Missouri and the peace of the frontier would be endangered, took immediate measures to check the evil.

With a detachment of the regiment stationed at the Bluffs he successfully attacked the Ricaree village, and it is hoped that such an impression has been made on them as well as on the other tribes on the Missouri as will prevent a recurrence of future hostility.

The report of the Secretary of War, which is herewith transmitted, will exhibit in greater detail the condition of the Department in its various branches, and the progress which has been made in its administration during the three first quarters of the year.

I transmit a return of the militia of the several States according to the last reports which have been made by the proper officers in each to the Department of War. By reference to this return it will be seen that it is not complete, although great exertions have been made to make it so. As the defense and even the liberties of the country must depend in times of imminent danger on the militia, it is of the highest importance that it be well organized, armed, and disciplined throughout the Union. The report of the Secretary of War shews the progress made during the three first quarters of the present year by the application of the fund appropriated for arming the militia. Much difficulty is found in distributing the arms according to the act of Congress providing for it from the failure of the proper departments in many of the States to make regular returns. The act of May 12, 1820, provides that the system of tactics and regulations of the various corps of the Regular Army shall be extended to the militia. This act has been very imperfectly executed from the want of uniformity in the organization of the militia, proceeding from the defects of the system itself, and especially in its application to that main arm of the public defense. It is thought that this important subject in all its branches merits the attention of Congress.

The report of the Secretary of the Navy which is now communicated, furnishes an account of the administration of that Department for the three first quarters of the present year, with the progress made in augmenting the Navy, and the manner in which the vessels in commission have been employed.

The usual force has been maintained in the Mediterranean Sea, the Pacific Ocean, and along the Atlantic coast, and has afforded the necessary protection to our commerce in those seas.

In the West Indies and the Gulf of Mexico our naval force has been augmented by the addition of several small vessels provided for by the "act authorizing an additional naval force for the suppression of piracy," passed by Congress at their last session. That armament has been eminently successful in the accomplishment of its object. The piracies by which our commerce in the neighborhood of the island of Cuba had been afflicted have been repressed and the confidence of our merchants in a great measure restored.

The patriotic zeal and enterprise of Commodore Porter, to whom the command of the expedition was confided, has been fully seconded by the officers and men under his command. And in reflecting with high satisfaction on the honorable manner in which they have sustained the reputation of their country and its Navy, the sentiment is alloyed only by a concern that in the fulfillment of that arduous service the diseases incident to the season and to the climate in which it was discharged have deprived the nation of many useful lives, and among them of several officers of great promise.

In the month of August a very malignant fever made its appearance at Thompsons Island, which threatened the destruction of our station there. Many perished, and the commanding officer was severely attacked. Uncertain as to his fate and knowing that most of the medical officers had been rendered incapable of discharging their duties, it was thought expedient to send to that post an officer of rank and experience, with several skillful surgeons, to ascertain the origin of the fever and the probability of its recurrence there in future seasons; to furnish every assistance to those who were suffering, and, if practicable, to avoid the necessity of abandoning so important a station. Commodore Rodgers, with a promptitude which did him honor, cheerfully accepted that trust, and has discharged it in the manner anticipated from his skill and patriotism. Before his arrival Commodore Porter, with the greater part of the squadron, had removed from the island and returned to the United States in consequence of the prevailing sickness. Much useful information has, however, been obtained as to the state of the island and great relief afforded to those who had been necessarily left there.

Although our expedition, cooperating with an invigorated administration of the government of the island of Cuba, and with the corresponding active exertions of a British naval force in the same seas, have almost entirely destroyed the unlicensed piracies from that island, the success of our exertions has not been equally effectual to suppress the same crime, under other pretenses and colors, in the neighboring island of Puerto Rico,

They have been committed there under the abusive issue of Spanish commissions. At an early period of the present year remonstrances were made to the governor of that island, by an agent who was sent for the purpose, against those outrages on the peaceful commerce of the United States, of which many had occurred. That officer, professing his own want of authority to make satisfaction for our just complaints, answered only by a reference of them to the Government of Spain. The minister of the United States to that court was specially instructed to urge the necessity of the immediate and effectual interposition of that Government, directing restitution and indemnity for wrongs already committed and interdicting the repetition of them. The minister, as has been seen, was debarred access to the Spanish Government, and in the meantime several new cases of flagrant outrage have occurred, and citizens of the United States in the island of Puerto Rico have suffered, and others been threatened with assassination for asserting their unquestionable rights even before the lawful tribunals of the country.

The usual orders have been given to all our public ships to seize American vessels engaged in the slave trade and bring them in for adjudication, and I have the gratification to state that not one so employed has been discovered, and there is good reason to believe that our flag is now seldom, if at all, disgraced by that traffic.

It is a source of great satisfaction that we are always enabled to recur to the conduct of our Navy with pride and commendation. As a means of national defense it enjoys the public confidence, and is steadily assuming additional importance. It is submitted whether a more efficient and equally economical organization of it might not in several respects be effected. It is supposed that higher grades than now exist by law would be useful. They would afford well-merited rewards to those who have long and faithfully served their country, present the best incentive to good conduct, and the best means of insuring a proper discipline; destroy the inequality in that respect between military and naval services, and relieve our officers from many inconveniences and mortifications which occur when our vessels meet those of other nations, ours being the only service in which such grades do not exist.

A report of the Postmaster-General, which accompanies this communication, will shew the present state of the Post-Office Department and its general operations for some years past.

There is established by law 88,600 miles of post-roads, on which the mail is now transported 85,700 miles, and contracts have been made for its transportation on all the established routes, with one or two exceptions. There are 5,240 post-offices in the Union, and as many postmasters. The gross amount of postage which accrued from the 1st July. 1822, to the 1st July, 1823, was $1,114,345.12. During the same period the expenditures of the Post-Office Department amounted to $1,169,885.51, and consisted of the following items, viz: Compensation to postmasters, $353,995.98; incidental expenses, $30,866.37; transportation of the mail,

$784,600.08; payments into the Treasury, $423.08. On the 1st of July last there was due to the Department from postmasters $135,245.28; from late postmasters and contractors, $256,749.31; making a total amount of balances due to the Department of $391,994.59. These balances embrace all delinquencies of postmasters and contractors which have taken place since the organization of the Department. There was due by the Department to contractors on the 1st of July last $26,548.64.

The transportation of the mail within five years past has been greatly extended, and the expenditures of the Department proportionably increased. Although the postage which has accrued within the last three years has fallen short of the expenditures $262,821.46, it appears that collections have been made from the outstanding balances to meet the principal part of the current demands.

It is estimated that not more than $250,000 of the above balances can be collected, and that a considerable part of this sum can only be realized by a resort to legal process. Some improvement in the receipts for postage is expected. A prompt attention to the collection of moneys received by postmasters, it is believed, will enable the Department to continue its operations without aid from the Treasury, unless the expenditures shall be increased by the establishment of new mail routes.

A revision of some parts of the post-office law may be necessary; and it is submitted whether it would not be proper to provide for the appointment of postmasters, where the compensation exceeds a certain amount, by nomination to the Senate, as other officers of the General Government are appointed.

Having communicated my views to Congress at the commencement of the last session respecting the encouragement which ought to be given to our manufactures and the principle on which it should be founded, I have only to add that those views remain unchanged, and that the present state of those countries with which we have the most immediate political relations and greatest commercial intercourse tends to confirm them. Under this impression I recommend a review of the tariff for the purposes of affording such additional protection to those articles which we are prepared to manufacture, or which are more immediately connected with the defense and independence of the country.

The actual state of the public accounts furnishes additional evidence of the efficiency of the present system of accountability in relation to the public expenditure. Of the moneys drawn from the Treasury since the 4th March, 1817, the sum remaining unaccounted for on the 30th of September last is more than a million and a half of dollars less than on the 30th of September preceding; and during the same period a reduction of nearly a million of dollars has been made in the amount of the unsettled accounts for moneys advanced previously to the 4th of March, 1817. It will be obvious that in proportion as the mass of accounts of the latter description is diminished by settlement the difficulty of settling the residue is increased from the consideration that in many instances it can be obtained only by legal process. For more precise details on this subject I refer to a report from the First Comptroller of the Treasury.

The sum which was appropriated at the last session for the repairs of the Cumberland road has been applied with good effect to that object. A final report has not yet been received from the agent who was appointed to superintend it. As soon as it is received it shall be communicated to Congress.

Many patriotic and enlightened citizens who have made the subject an object of particular investigation have suggested an improvement of still greater importance. They are of opinion that the waters of the Chesapeake and Ohio may be connected together by one continued canal, and at an expense far short of the value and importance of the object to be obtained. If this could be accomplished it is impossible to calculate the beneficial consequences which would result from it. A great portion of the produce of the very fertile country through which it would pass would find a market through that channel. Troops might be moved with great facility in war, with cannon and every kind of munition, and in either direction. Connecting the Atlantic with the Western country in a line passing through the seat of the National Government, it would contribute essentially to strengthen the bond of union itself. Believing as I do that Congress possess the right to appropriate money for such a national object (the jurisdiction remaining to the States through which the canal would pass), I submit it to your consideration whether it may not be advisable to authorize by an adequate appropriation the employment of a suitable number of the officers of the Corps of Engineers to examine the unexplored ground during the next season and to report their opinion thereon. It will likewise be proper to extend their examination to the several routes through which the waters of the Ohio may be connected by canals with those of Lake Erie.

As the Cumberland road will require annual repairs, and Congress have not thought it expedient to recommend to the States an amendment to the Constitution for the purpose of vesting in the United States a power to adopt and execute a system of internal improvement, it is also submitted to your consideration whether it may not be expedient to authorize the Executive to enter into an arrangement with the several States through which the road passes to establish tolls, each within its limits, for the purpose of defraying the expense of future repairs and of providing also by suitable penalties for its protection against future injuries.

The act of Congress of the 7th of May, 1822, appropriated the sum of $22,700 for the purpose of erecting two piers as a shelter for vessels from ice near Cape Henlopen, Delaware Bay. To effect the object of the act the officers of the Board of Engineers, with Commodore Bainbridge, were directed to prepare plans and estimates of piers sufficient to answer the purpose intended by the act. It appears by their report, which accompanies the documents from the War Department, that the appropriation is not adequate to the purpose intended; and as the piers would be of great service both to the navigation of the Delaware Bay and the protection of vessels on the adjacent parts of the coast, I submit for the consideration of Congress whether additional and sufficient appropriation should not be made.

The Board of Engineers were also directed to examine and survey the entrance of the harbor of the port of Presquille, in Pennsylvania, in order to make an estimate of the expense of removing the obstructions to the entrance, with a plan of the best mode of effecting the same, under the appropriation for that purpose by act of Congress passed 3d of March last. The report of the Board accompanies the papers from the War Department, and is submitted for the consideration of Congress.

A strong hope has been long entertained, founded on the heroic struggle of the Greeks, that they would succeed in their contest and resume their equal station among the nations of the earth. It is believed that the whole civilized world take a deep interest in their welfare. Although no power has declared in their favor, yet none, according to our information, has taken part against them. Their cause and their name have protected them from dangers which might ere this have overwhelmed any other people. The ordinary calculations of interest and of acquisition with a view to aggrandizement, which mingles so much in the transactions of nations, seems to have had no effect in regard to them. From the facts which have come to our knowledge there is good cause to believe that their enemy has lost forever all dominion over them; that Greece will become again an independent nation. That she may obtain that rank is the object of our most ardent wishes.

It was stated at the commencement of the last session that a great effort was then making in Spain and Portugal to improve the condition of the people of those countries, and that it appeared to be conducted with extraordinary moderation. It need scarcely be remarked that the result has been so far very different from what was then anticipated. Of events in that quarter of the globe, with which we have so much intercourse and from which we derive our origin, we have always been anxious and interested spectators. The citizens of the United States cherish sentiments the most friendly in favor of the liberty and happiness of their fellow-men on that side of the Atlantic. In the wars of the European powers in matters relating to themselves we have never taken any part, nor does it comport with our policy to do so. It is only when our rights are invaded or seriously menaced that we resent injuries or make preparation for our defense. With the movements in this hemisphere we are of necessity more immediately connected, and by causes which must be obvious to all enlightened and impartial observers. The political system of the allied powers is essentially different in this respect from that of America. This difference proceeds from that which exists in their respective Governments; and to the defense of our own, which has been achieved by the loss of so much blood and treasure, and matured by the wisdom of their most enlightened citizens, and under which we have enjoyed unexampled felicity, this whole nation is devoted. We owe it, therefore, to candor and to the amicable relations existing between the United States and those powers to declare that we should consider any attempt on their part to extend their system to any portion of this hemisphere as dangerous to our peace and safety. With the existing colonies or dependencies of any European power we have not interfered and shall not interfere. But with the Governments who have declared their independence and maintained it, and whose independence we have, on great consideration and on just principles, acknowledged, we could not view any interposition for the purpose of oppressing them, or controlling in any other manner their destiny, by any European power in any other light than as the manifestation of an unfriendly disposition toward the United States. In the war between those new Governments and Spain we declared our neutrality at the time of their recognition, and to this we have adhered, and shall continue to adhere, provided no change shall occur which, in the judgment of the competent authorities of this Government, shall make a corresponding change on the part of the United States indispensable to their security.

The late events in Spain and Portugal shew that Europe is still unsettled. Of this important fact no stronger proof can be adduced than that the allied powers should have thought it proper, on any principle satisfactory to themselves, to have interposed by force in the internal concerns of Spain. To what extent such interposition may be carried, on the same principle, is a question in which all independent powers whose governments differ from theirs are interested, even those most remote, and surely none more so than the United States. Our policy in regard to Europe, which was adopted at an early stage of the wars which have so long agitated that quarter of the globe, nevertheless remains the same, which is, not to interfere in the internal concerns of any of its powers; to consider the government **de facto** as the legitimate government for us; to cultivate friendly relations with it, and to preserve those relations by a frank, firm, and manly policy, meeting in all instances the just claims of every power, submitting to injuries from none. But in regard to those continents circumstances are eminently and conspicuously different. It is impossible that the allied powers should extend their political system to any portion of either continent without endangering our peace and happiness; nor can anyone believe that our southern brethren, if left to themselves, would adopt it of their own accord. It is equally impossible, therefore, that we should behold such interposition in any form with indifference. If we look to the comparative strength and resources of Spain and those new Governments, and their distance from each other, it must be obvious that she can never subdue them. It is still the true policy of the

United States to leave the parties to themselves, in the hope that other powers will pursue the same course.

If we compare the present condition of our Union with its actual state at the close of our Revolution, the history of the world furnishes no example of a progress in improvement in all the important circumstances which constitute the happiness of a nation which bears any resemblance to it. At the first epoch our population did not exceed 3,000,000. By the last census it amounted to about 10,000,000, and, what is more extraordinary, it is almost altogether native, for the immigration from other countries has been inconsiderable. At the first epoch half the territory within our acknowledged limits was uninhabited and a wilderness. Since then new territory has been acquired of vast extent, comprising within it many rivers, particularly the Mississippi, the navigation of which to the ocean was of the highest importance to the original States. Over this territory our population has expanded in every direction, and new States have been established almost equal in number to those which formed the first bond of our Union. This expansion of our population and accession of new States to our Union have had the happiest effect on all its highest interests. That it has eminently augmented our resources and added to our strength and respectability as a power is admitted by all. But it is not in these important circumstances only that this happy effect is felt. It is manifest that by enlarging the basis of our system and increasing the number of States the system itself has been greatly strengthened in both its branches. Consolidation and disunion have thereby been rendered equally impracticable. Each Government, confiding in its own strength, has less to apprehend from the other, and in consequence each, enjoying a greater freedom of action, is rendered more efficient for all the purposes for which it was instituted. It is unnecessary to treat here of the vast improvement made in the system itself by the adoption of this Constitution and of its happy effect in elevating the character and in protecting the rights of the nation as well as of individuals. To what, then, do we owe these blessings? It is known to all that we derive them from the excellence of our institutions. Ought we not, then, to adopt every measure which may be necessary to perpetuate them?

JAMES MONROE.

MESSAGE ON ESTABLISHMENT
OF PEACE TIME NAVY
January 30, 1824

*On December 15, 1823, the House of Representatives
passed a resolution calling upon the President to
"communicate a plan for the peace establishment of
the Navy of the United States." The following was
his response.*

The the House of Representatives of the United States:

In compliance with a resolution of the House of Representatives of the
15th of December last, requesting the President of the United States "to
communicate a plan for a peace establishment of the Navy of the United
States," I herewith transmit a report from the Secretary of the Navy,
which contains the plan required.

In presenting this plan to the consideration of Congress, I avail myself
of the occasion to make some remarks on it which the importance of the
subject requires and experience justifies.

If a system of universal and permanent peace could be established, or
if in war the belligerent parties would respect the rights of neutral powers, we should have no occasion for a navy or an army. The expense and
dangers of such establishments might be avoided. The history of all ages
proves that this can not be presumed; on the contrary, that at least one-
half of every century, in ancient as well as modern times, has been con-
sumed in wars, and often of the most general and desolating character.
Nor is there any cause to infer, if we examine the condition of the nations with which we have the most intercourse and strongest political
relations, that we shall in future be exempt from that calamity within any
period to which a rational calculation may be extended. And as to the
rights of neutral powers, it is sufficient to appeal to our own experience
to demonstrate how little regard will be paid to them whenever they
come in conflict with the interests of the powers at war while we rely
on the justice of our cause and on argument alone. The amount of the
property of our fellow-citizens which was seized and confiscated or destroyed by the belligerent parties in the wars of the French Revolution,
and of those which followed before we became a party to the war,
is almost incalculable.

The whole movement of our Government from the establishment of
our independence has been guided by a sacred regard for peace. Situated
as we are in the new hemisphere, distant from Europe and unconnected
with its affairs, blessed with the happiest Government on earth, and hav-

ing no objects of ambition to gratify, the United States have steadily cultivated the relations of amity with every power; and if in any European wars a respect for our rights might be relied on, it was undoubtedly in those to which I have adverted. The conflict being vital, the force being nearly equally balanced, and the result uncertain, each party had the strongest motives of interest to cultivate our good will, lest we might be thrown into the opposite scale. Powerful as this consideration usually is, it was nevertheless utterly disregarded in almost every stage of and by every party to those wars. To these encroachments and injuries our regard for peace was finally forced to yield.

In the war to which at length we became a party our whole coast from St. Croix to the Mississippi was either invaded or menaced with invasion, and in many parts with a strong imposing force both land and naval. In those parts where the population was most dense the pressure was comparatively light, but there was scarcely an harbor or city on any of our great inlets which could be considered secure. New York and Philadelphia were eminently exposed, the then existing works not being sufficient for their protection. The same remark is applicable in a certain extent to the cities eastward of the former, and as to the condition of the whole country southward of the latter the events which mark the war are too recent to require detail. Our armies and Navy signalized themselves in every quarter where they had occasion to meet their gallant foe, and the militia voluntarily flew to their aid with a patriotism and fought with a bravery which exalted the reputation of their Government and country and which did them the highest honor. In whatever direction the enemy chose to move with their squadrons and to land their troops our fortifications, where any existed, presented but little obstacle to them. They passed those works without difficulty. Their squadrons, in fact, annoyed our whole coast, not of the sea only, but every bay and great river throughout its whole extent. In entering those inlets and sailing up them with a small force the effect was disastrous, since it never failed to draw out the whole population on each side and to keep it in the field while the squadron remained there. The expense attending this species of defense, with the exposure of the inhabitants and the waste of property, may readily be conceived.

The occurrences which preceded the war and those which attended it, were alike replete with useful instruction as to our future policy. Those which marked the first epoch demonstrate clearly that in the wars of other powers we can rely only on force for the protection of our neutral rights. Those of the second demonstrate with equal certainty that in any war in which we may be engaged hereafter with a strong naval power the expense, waste, and other calamities attending it, considering the vast extent of our maritime frontier, can not fail, unless it be defended by adequate fortifications and a suitable naval force, to correspond with those which were experienced in the late war. Two great objects are therefore to be regarded in the establishment of an adequate naval force: The first, to prevent war so far as it may be practicable; the second, to diminish its calamities when it may be inevitable. Hence the subject of defense becomes intimately connected in all its parts in war and in peace, for the land and at sea. No government will be disposed in its wars with other powers to violate our rights if it knows we have the means, are prepared and resolved to defend them. The motive will also be diminished if it knows that our defenses by land are so well planned and executed that an invasion of our coast can not be productive of the evils to which we have heretofore been exposed.

It was under a thorough conviction of these truths, derived from the admonitions of the late war, that Congress, as early as the year 1816, during the term of my enlightened and virtuous predecessor, under whom the war had been declared, prosecuted, and terminated, digested and made provision for the defense of our country and support of its rights, in peace as well as in war, by acts which authorized and enjoined the augmentation of our Navy to a prescribed limit, and the construction of suitable fortifications throughout the whole extent of our maritime frontier and wherever else they might be deemed necessary. It is to the execution of these works, both land and naval, and under a thorough conviction that by hastening their completion I should render the best service to my country and give the most effectual support to our free republican system of government that my humble faculties would admit of, that I have devoted so much of my time and labor to this great system of national policy since I came into this office, and shall continue to do it until my retirement from it at the end of your next session.

The Navy is the arm from which our Government will always derive most aid in support of our neutral rights. Every power engaged in war will know the strength of our naval force, the number of our ships of each class, their condition, and the promptitude with which we may bring them into service, and will pay due consideration to that argument. Justice will always have great weight in the cabinets of Europe; but in long and destructive wars exigencies often occur which press so vitally on them that unless the argument of force is brought to its aid it will be disregarded. Our land forces will always perform their duty in the event of war, but they must perform it on the land. Our Navy is the arm which must be principally relied on for the annoyance of the commerce of the enemy and for the protection of our own, and also, by cooperation with the land forces, for the defense of the country. Capable of moving in any and every direction, it possesses the faculty, even when remote from our coast, of extending its aid to every interest on which the security and welfare of our Union depend. Annoying the commerce of the enemy and menacing in turn its coast, provided the force on each side is nearly equally balanced, it will draw its squadrons from our own; and in case of invasion by a powerful adversary by a land and naval force, which is always to be anticipated and ought to be provided against, our Navy may, by like cooperation with our land forces, render essential aid in protecting our interior from incursion and depredation.

The great object in the event of war is to stop the enemy at the coast. If this is done our cities and whole interior will be secure. For the accomplishment of this object our fortifications must be principally relied on. By placing strong works near the mouths of our great inlets in such positions as to command the entrances into them, as may be done in many instances, it will be difficult, if not impossible, for ships to pass them, especially if other precautions, and particularly that of steam batteries, are resorted to in their aid. In the wars between other powers into which we may be drawn in support of our neutral rights it can not be doubted that this defense would be adequate to the purpose intended by it, nor can it be doubted that the knowledge that such works existed would form a strong motive with any power not to invade our rights, and thereby contribute essentially to prevent war. There are, it is admitted, some entrances into our interior which are of such vast extent that it would be utterly impossible for any works, however extensive or well posted, to command them. Of this class the Chesapeake Bay, which is an arm of the sea, may be given as an example. But, in my judgment, even this bay may be defended against any power with whom we may be involved in war as a third party in the defense of our neutral rights. By erecting strong works at the mouth of James River, on both sides, near the capes, as we are now doing, and at Old Point Comfort and the Rip Raps, and connecting those works together by chains whenever the enemy's force appeared, placing in the rear some large ships and steam batteries, the passage up the river would be rendered impracticable. This guard would also tend to protect the whole country bordering on the bay and rivers emptying into it, as the hazard would be too great for the enemy, however strong his naval force, to ascend the bay and leave such a naval force behind; since, in the event of a storm, whereby his vessels might be separated, or of a calm, the ships and steam batteries behind the works might rush forth and destroy them. It could only be in the event of an invasion by a great power or a combination of several powers, and by land as well as by naval forces, that those works could be carried; and even then they could not fail to retard the movement of the enemy into the country and to give time for the collection of our regular troops, militia, and volunteers to that point, and thereby contribute essentially to his ultimate defeat and expulsion from our territory.

Under a strong impression that a peace establishment of our Navy is connected with the possible event of war, and that the naval force intended for either state, however small it may be, is connected with the general system of public defense, I have thought it proper in communicating this report to submit these remarks on the whole subject.

JAMES MONROE.

REQUEST TO CONGRESS FOR SETTLEMENT
OF PERSONAL CLAIMS
January 5, 1825

A few months prior to the end of his second term as President, Monroe appealed to Congress to settle outstanding claims which he felt were owed to him by the government. According to Monroe, he had paid out of his own pocket many expenses incurred during his diplomatic missions to France, England and Spain. Despite this appeal, Congress was less than generous in its treatment of Monroe. Although he was forced to sell much of his personal property to satisfy creditors, Congress delayed any kind of settlement until a few months prior to his death in 1825, when he was awarded $30,000 in partial settlement. Ironically enough, although both Monroe and Jefferson lived their final years in far from prosperous circumstances, Congress voted (in December, 1824) to give Lafayette "200,000 in money and a township of public land."

To the Senate and House of Representatives of the United States

As the term of my service in this high trust will expire at the end of the present session of Congress, I think it proper to invite your attention to an object very interesting to me, and which in the movement of our Government is deemed on principle equally interesting to the public. I have been long in the service of my country and in its most difficult conjunctures, as well abroad as at home, in the course of which I have had a control over the public moneys to a vast amount. If in the course of my service it shall appear on the most severe scrutiny, which I invite, that the public have sustained any loss by any act of mine, or of others for which I ought to be held responsible, I am willing to bear it. If, on the other hand, it shall appear on a view of the law and of precedents in other cases that justice has been withheld from me in any instance, as I have believed it to be in many, and greatly to my injury, it is submitted whether it ought not to be rendered. It is my wish that all matters of account and claims between my country and myself be settled with that strict regard to justice which is observed in settlements between individuals in private life. It would be gratifying to me, and it appears to be just, that the subject should be now examined in both respects with a view to a decision hereafter. No bill would, it is presumed, be presented for my signature which would operate either for or against me, and I would certainly sanction none in my favor. While here I can furnish testimony, applicable to any case, in both views, while a full investigation may require, and the committee to whom the subject may be referred, by reporting facts now with a view to a decision after my retirement, will allow time for further information and due consideration of all matters relating thereto. Settlements with a person in this trust, which could not be made with the accounting officers of the Government, should always be made by Congress and before the public. The cause of the delay in presenting these claims will be explained to the committee to whom the subject may be referred. It will, I presume, be made apparent that it was inevitable; that from the peculiar circumstances attending each case Congress alone could decide on it, and that from considerations of delicacy it would have been highly improper for me to have sought it from Congress at an earlier period than that which is now proposed— the expiration of my term in this high trust.

Other considerations appear to me to operate with great force in favor of the measure which I now propose. A citizen who has long served his country in its highest trusts has a right, if he has served with fidelity, to enjoy undisturbed tranquillity and peace in his retirement. This he can not expect to do unless his conduct in all pecuniary concerns shall be placed by severe scrutiny on a basis not to be shaken. This, therefore, forms a strong motive with me for the inquiry which I now invite. The public may also derive considerable advantage from the precedent in the future movement of the Government. It being known that such scrutiny was made in my case, it may form a new and strong barrier against the abuse of the public confidence in future.

                                        JAMES MONROE.

FAREWELL TO JAMES MADISON
April 11, 1831

This letter to President Madison, written some three months before his death, from New York, the home of his daughter and son-in-law, shows Monroe to be in ill health and forced to sell his property in Virginia in order to raise money. Monroe complains once again about the unwillingness of Congress to reimburse him fully for the money he spent during his diplomatic service in Europe. In his reply, dated April 21, 1831, Madison noted that Congress had just voted to compensate Monroe with a sum somewhat larger than that recommended by the accounting officers.

Dear Sir,—I have intended for some time to write and explain to you the arrangement I have made for my future residence, and respecting my private affairs, with a view to my comfort, so far as I may expect it, but it has been painful to me to execute it. My ill state of health continuing, consisting of a cough, which annoys me by night and by day into considerable expectoration, considering my advanced years, although my lungs are not affected, renders the restoration of my health very uncertain, or indeed any favorable change in it. In such a state I could not reside on my farm. The solitude would be very distressing, and its cares very burthensome. It is the wish of both my daughters, and of the whole connection, that I should remain here & receive their good offices, which I have decided to do. I do not wish to burthen them. It is my intention to rent a house near Mr. Gouveneur, and to live within my own resources, so far as I may be able. I could make no establishment of any kind without the sale of my property in Loudon, which I have advertised for the 8th of June, and given the necessary power to Mr. Gouveneur & my nephew James. If my health will permit I will visit it in the interim, to arrange affairs there for that event, and my removal here. The accounting officers have made no decision in my claims & have given me much trouble. I have told them that I would make out no account adapted to the act, which fell far short of making me a just reparation, and that I had rather lose the whole sum than give to it any sanction, be the consequences what they may. I never recovered from the losses of the first mission, to which those of the second added considerably.

It is very distressing to me to sell my property in Loudon, for, besides parting with all I have in the State, I indulged a hope, if I could retain it, that I might be able occasionally to visit it, and meet my friends, or many of them there. But ill health & advanced years prescribe a course which we must pursue. I deeply regret that there is no prospect of our ever meeting again, since so long have we been connected, and in the most friendly intercourse, in public & private life, that a final separation is among the most distressing incidents which could occur. I shall resign my seat as a visitor at the Board in due time to enable the Executive to fill the vacancy that my successor may attend the next meeting. I beg you to assure Mrs. Madison that I can never forget the friiendly relation which has existed between her and my family. We often remind us of incidents of the most interesting character. My daughter, Mrs. Hay, will live with me, who with the whole family here unite in affectionate regards to both of you.

JAMES MONROE

REPUDIATION OF THE RHEA LETTER
June 19, 1831

Fifteen days before his death, Monroe wrote what is almost certainly his last public document—a repudiation of the insinuations of John Rhea. In this deposition, which was sworn to before two witnesses, Monroe states emphatically that he had never authorized John Rhea to write a letter to Andrew Jackson, authorizing him to disobey orders he had already been given in regard to Florida. The fact that this document is virtually a "deathbed" statement lends weight to the belief that Monroe was innocent of any complicity in the controversy. In this document, Monroe says that his son-in-law, Samuel Gouveneur, had kept the letter from him "for reasons which he will explain." Gouveneuer later revealed that he had withheld the Rhea letter because Monroe was in ill health and had been confined to bed for several weeks.

A letter of John Rhea of Tennessee is shown to me this nineteenth day of June, 1831, for the first time, nor have I previously had any intimation of the receipt of such a letter or of its contents. It was received by Mrs. Gouveneur, as I am told by him, and after having been read, kept from me, for reasons which he will explain, until this time. Had it been communicated to me before, I should have made, as I do now do, the following declaration & reply thereto, which I wish to be filed with the said letter, as my reply to its contents.

1st. It is utterly unfounded & untrue that I ever authorized John Rhea to write any letter whatever to Genl. Jackson, authorizing or encouraging him to disobey, or deviate from the orders which had been communicated to him from the Department of War.

2nd. That it is utterly unfounded & untrue that I ever desired the said John Rhea to request Genl. Jackson to destroy any letter written by him, the said John Rhea to Genl. Jackson, nor did I at any time wish or desire that any letter, document, or memorandum, in the possession of Genl. Jackson, or of any other person, relating to my official conduct, in respect of the Seminole War, or any other public matter, should be destroyed.

A note applicable to this subject will be found among my papers at Oak Hill in Virginia, to which as well as to my whole correspondence with General Jackson, as well as others, I refer, for the truth of this statement.

JAMES MONROE

BIBLIOGRAPHICAL AIDS

The emphasis in this and subsequent volumes in the **Presidential Chronologies** will be on the administrations of the presidents. The more important works on other aspects of their lives, either before or after their terms, are included since they may contribute to an understanding of the presidential careers.

The following bibliography is critically selected. Many additional titles may be found in the works by Cresson and Gilman (see below) and in the standard guide. The student might also wish to consult **Reader's Guide to Periodical Literature** and **Social Sciences and Humanities Index** (formerly **International Index**) for recent articles in scholarly journals.

Additional chronological information not included in this volume because it did not relate directly to the president may be found in the **Encyclopedia of American History**, edited by Richard B. Morris, revised edition (New York, 1965).

Asterisks after titles refer to books currently available in paperback editions.

SOURCE MATERIALS

Published literature by and about James Monroe is, unfortunately, definitely on the spare side. Monroe himself wrote relatively little about the more important events of his life. For the most part, his writings are taken up with defenses of those actions in his life which most aroused public criticism: i.e., his diplomatic missions to Europe, his part in the notorious "Reynolds Affair," and his financial claims against the United States government.

Nor are the historical writings of other authors much better when it comes to dealing with Monroe's presidency as a whole. For example, only a few full length biographies have been published—none of them multi-volume and none what might be described as "definitive" works. The great bulk of literature about Monroe tends to concentrate upon specific events in his administration: i.e., the Monroe Doctrine, the Era of Good Feelings, and so on. The net effect of this "fragmentary" approach is obvious—the serious student is often hard put to place James Monroe in proper perspective. All too often, a book about Monroe means really an in-depth study of one or two years of his administration.

One other problem faces students bent on reading about Monroe: a near famine of recent publications about the man and his presidency. A quick glance through a library catalog will bear out the fact that many, if not most, books on Monroe were written at least 40 years ago. Readers should bear in mind that these books, excellent as they have been in their time, bear the stamp of another era's prejudices and outlook.

Brown, Stuart Gerry, ed. **The Autobiography of James Monroe.** Syra-
cuse, 1959. This book can best be described as massive fragments
of an autobiography. Although Monroe touches upon his military
experience, law education, and training as an aide to Jefferson,
almost one-half of the book is devoted to Monroe's first controver-
sial mission to France. Monroe writes in a ponderous style; nevertheless, the book is frequently instructive. The account ends in 1807,
when Monroe was 49 years old.

Hamilton, S.M., ed. **The Writings of James Monroe.** 8 vols. New York,
1898-1903. These volumes are invaluable for a study of Monroe and
his times.

Monroe, James. **A View of the Conduct of the Executive, in the Foreign
Affairs of the United States, connected with the mission to the French
Republic, during the years 1794, 5 & 6.** Charlottesville, 1797. This
tract of more than 100 pages was written as a justification of Monroe's first diplomatic mission to France. It is hardly a model of ob-
jectivity. There is a certain amount of judicious .omission of facts
prejudicial to Monroe's side of the controversy; the interpretation of
facts is also highly colored by Monroe. The tract ends with a bitter
denunciation of President Washington's policy.

—————— **Observations on Certain Documents contained in Nos. V
and VI of "The History of the United States for the year 1796."
in which the Charge of Speculation against Alexander Hamilton, late
Secretary of the Treasury, is fully refuted.** Philadelphia, 1797. This is
Monroe's version of the "Reynolds Affair."

—————— **Memoir of James Monroe, Esq. Relating to His Unsettled
Claims upon The People and Government of the United States.**
Charlottesville, 1828. Here, Monroe presents his case for the money
which he claimed the United States owed him for expenses during
his diplomatic missions.

BIOGRAPHIES

Adams, John Quincy. **The Lives of James Madison and James Monroe.**
Buffalo, 1850. Perhaps the outstanding asset of this account is that
it is one of the few written by a contemporary of Monroe's.

Cresson, William P. **James Monroe.** Chapel Hill, 1946. This detailed
biography has the virtue of being eminently readable—and the fault
of being somewhat biased in favor of Monroe. Doubtful actions on
Monroe's part—for example, his behavior in the "Reynolds Affair"
or his diplomatic skill in France—are smoothed over by the author.
All too often, other political figures are made the scapegoat for

Monroe's mistakes. Nevertheless, this biography provides one of the best sources for a general picture of Monroe.

Gilman, Daniel C. **James Monroe.** Boston, 1883. Although thin and dated, this biography does provide one valuable asset—a bibliography of writings pertinent to the Monroe Doctrine (compiled by John F. Jameson).

Morgan, George. **The Life of James Monroe.** Boston, 1921. Useful for Monroe's early life but not of much value for his career as either Secretary of State or as President.

Styron, Arthur. **The Last of the Cocked Hats: James Monroe and the Virginia Dynasty.** Norman, Okla., 1945. A worthwhile and solid biography, with emphasis on the time and environment in which Monroe lived.

SPECIAL AREAS

Brown, Everett Sommerville, ed. **The Missouri Compromise and Presidential Politics, 1820-1825.** St. Louis, 1926.

Cresson, W.P. **The Holy Alliance: The European Background of the Monroe Doctrine.** New York, 1922. An examination of European politics on the heels of Napoleon's defeat and of those international intrigues which led to the formulation of the Monroe Doctrine.

Dangerfield, George. **The Awakening of American Nationalism: 1815-1818.** New York, 1965. This book examines many of the important events of Monroe's administration, particularly as they relate to the growing nationalism of America.

—————— **The Era of Good Feelings.** New York, 1952.* Covers the period from 1814 to 1829, which includes the latter part of Madison's term, John Quincy Adam's term and both of Monroe's terms. It is essentially a description of some of the personalities and experiences, both American and European, which figured in the political transition from Jeffersonian to Jacksonian democracy. Reliable and interesting.

Perkins, Dexter. **The Monroe Doctrine, 1823-1826.** Harvard Historical Studies, Vol. XXIX. Cambridge, 1927. An account by one of America's foremost historians.

ESSAYS

Perkins, Dexter. "John Quincy Adams," in **The American Secretaries of State and Their Diplomacy.** Vol. IV. Edited by S. F. Bemis (New York, 1928).

0

Pratt, Julius W. "James Monroe," in **The American Secretaries of State and Their Diplomacy.** Vol. III. Edited by S. F. Bemis (New York, 1928).

Sydnor, Charles S. "The One-Party Period in American History," **American Historical Review,** LI (April, 1946), 439-451.

Also see Bibliography in Dangerfield, **The Era of Good Feelings,** already cited, as well as **Reader's Guide to Periodical Literature** and the **Social Sciences and Humanities Index** for newer treatments in scholarly journals.

THE PRESIDENCY

Bailey, Thomas A. **Presidential Greatness: The Image and the Man from George Washington to the Present.** New York, 1966.* A critical and subjective study of the qualities of presidential greatness, arranged topically rather than chronologically.

Binkley, Wilfred E. **The Man in the White House: His Powers and Duties.** Revised ed. New York, 1964.* Treats the development of the various roles of the American president.

Brown, Stuart Gerry. **The American Presidency: Leadership, Partisanship and Popularity.** New York, 1966. Seems to like the more partisan presidents like Jefferson and Jackson.

Corwin, Edward S. **The President: Office and Powers.** 4th ed. New York, 1957. An older classic.

Kane, Joseph Nathan. **Facts About the Presidents.** New York, 1959. Includes comparative as well as biographical data about the presidents.

Koenig, Louis W. **The Chief Executive.** New York, 1964. Authoritative study of presidential powers.

Laski, Harold J. **The American Presidency.** New York, 1940. A classic.

Rossiter, Clinton. **The American Presidency.** 2nd ed. New York, 1960. Somewhat useful.

Schlesinger, Arthur Meier. "Historians Rate United States Presidents," **Life,** XXV, November 1, 1948, 65ff.

—————— "Our Presidents: A Rating by Seventy-five Historians," **New York Times Magazine,** July 29, 1962, 12 ff.

NAME INDEX

Adams, John, 4, 7, 24
Adams, John Quincy, 13, 17, 19, 21, 22, 23, 24

Alexander, William (see Lord Stirling), 2

Allen, Herman, 21
Ambrister, Robert, 16
Arbuthnot, Alexander, 16
Armstrong, John, 12
Aury, Louis, 14
Bagot, Charles, 14, 15
Biddle, Nicholas, 22
Calhoun, John C., 14, 15, 16, 22, 23
Callava, Jose Maria, 19
Campbell, (Parson) Archibald, 1
Canning, George, 21
Castlereagh, Robert Stewart, 12
Clark, William, 8
Clay, Henry, 14, 17, 18, 22, 23
Clingman, Jacob, 5
Clinton, George, 10
Crawford, William Harris, 13, 22, 23
Crowinshield, Benjamin W., 14
Dunmore, Lord, 1
Edwards, Ninian, 22
Eustis, William, 12
Foster, A.J., 11
Fromentin (Judge) Elijius, 19
Gallatin, Albert, 16
Gardoqui, Don Diego de, 3

Gouveneur, Samuel Lawrence (son-in-law), 18, 24
Hamilton, Alexander, 5, 7
Harrison, William Henry, 11, 12
Hay, George (son-in-law), 10
Hull, (General) William, 12
Jackson, Andrew, 13, 15, 16, 17, 19, 20, 23, 24
Jay, John, 3
Jefferson, Thomas, 2, 7, 8, 9, 10, 21, 24
Jones, (Judge) Joseph, 1
Key, Francis Scott, 12
King, Rufus, 13
Kortright, Elizabeth (see also Mrs. James Monroe), 4
Kortright, Hannah Aspinwall, 4
Kortright, Lawrence, 4
Lafayette, Marquis de, 2, 6, 21, 23, 24
Lewis, Meriwether, 8
Livingston, R.R., 8
Macon, Nathaniel, 10
Madison, James, 9, 10, 11, 12, 21, 24
Marshall, John, 1, 4, 13, 17, 19, 24
McLean, John, 21
Meigs, Jonathan, Jr., 14
Monroe, Eliza Kortright (daughter; Mrs. George Hay), 4, 10
Monroe, Elizabeth Jones (mother), 1

85

TITLES IN THE OCEANA
PRESIDENTIAL CHRONOLOGY SERIES

Reference books containing Chronology — Documents — Bibliographical Aids for each President covered.

Series Editor: Howard F. Bremer

1.	GEORGE WASHINGTON edited by Howard F. Bremer	96 pages/$3.00
2.	JOHN ADAMS edited by Howard F. Bremer	96 pages/$3.00
3.	JAMES BUCHANAN edited by Irving J. Sloan	96 pages/$3.00
4.	GROVER CLEVELAND edited by Robert I. Vexler	128 pages/$4.00
5.	FRANKLIN PIERCE edited by Irving J. Sloan	96 pages/$3.00
6.	ULYSSES S. GRANT edited by Philip R. Moran	128 pages/$4.00
7.	MARTIN VAN BUREN edited by Irving J. Sloan	128 pages/$4.00
8.	THEODORE ROOSEVELT edited by Gilbert Black	128 pages/$4.00
9.	BENJAMIN HARRISON* edited by Harry J. Sievers	96 pages/$3.00
10.	JAMES MONROE edited by Ian Elliot	96 pages/$3.00
11.	WOODROW WILSON* edited by Robert Vexler	128 pages/$4.00
12.	RUTHERFORD B. HAYES edited by Arthur Bishop	96 pages/$3.00
13.	ANDREW JACKSON* edited by Ronald Shaw	128 pages/$4.00
14.	WARREN HARDING* edited by Philip Moran	96 pages/$3.00

*Available June, 1969

Books may be ordered from
OCEANA PUBLICATIONS, INC.
Dobbs Ferry, New York 10522